FISCAL POLICY IN NORTH-EAST INDIA

FISCAL POLICY IN NORTH-EAST INDIA

B. Mishra

AKANSHA PUBLISHING HOUSE
NEW DELHI-110002

AKANSHA PUBLISHING HOUSE
4649-B/21, Ansari Road
Darya Ganj, New Delhi - 110 002
Email: ektabooks@yahoo.com
Ph.: 23263193/9811582579
Fax: 011-23263193

Fiscal Policy in North-East India

First Published 2006
ISBN 81-8370-063-2

PRINTED IN INDIA

Published by M.P. Misra for Akansha Publishing House, New Delhi and Printed at Aryan Enterprises, Delhi

CONTENTS

PREFACE

Over a period of time, North-Eastern states have developed a dependency syndrome as it is evident from an explosive cycle of public expenditure growth in most of the states of the region, coupled with an increasing demand for grants-in-aids and other Central assistance to bridge the gap of large budgetary deficits. The inadequacy in generating their own sources of revenue to meet the challenge of a volatile fiscal situation may be attributed to a number of factors. They are : (i) the low level of economic activities coupled with a low level of economic base, which may be considered as a product of low level of infrastructural development (ii) emergence of a parallel economy not only due to flourishing trade of imported goods and commodities from the neighboring countries but also due to the various fringe tax benefits of direct taxation particularly of Income tax and lastly (iii) due to the social unrest and political instability that these economies experience from time to time. As a whole, the repercussion effects of all these forces at work has resulted in various leakages not only in tax generating capacity but also in narrowing down the tax base of various taxes in the region. If we are to assign a cause- effect relationship to this type of vexed problem then we can argue that the failures on the part of the state governments in this region to mobilize adequate financial resources in order to carry out their various developmental plan programs, has been mainly responsible for their low level of economic activities, low level of economic base and their final culmination in the form of social unrest. This poor state of affairs in the fiscal front of the North-Eastern states may be termed as *tribal fiscal dilemma* that haunts all the north-eastern states. In a welfare characterized state, fulfillment of social desire to have a better quality of life is dependent not only on the capacity of the government to mobilize adequate resources but also on the degree of momentum of the economic activities that a state in question attains. In the absence of a desired level of economic tolerance to the expanded economic activities, mobilizations of adequate resources for carrying out their developmental works are left to the mercy of the capacity of the government to mobilize adequate resources.

The book is an attempt to accomplish the above anomalies by analyzing fiscal position of Northeastern states from the angles of resource mobilization (level of revenue) and its utilization (level of public expenditure). By applying four indicators, viz. compound growth rate, marginal tax rates, and elasticity and buoyancy coefficients to the North-Eastern states tax structure, the present book tries to assess the fiscal performances of these states in terms of their problems and prospects to achieve a reasonable degree fiscal capacity to carry out their developmental works.

I hope that the present book will prove to be of immense value to the post-graduate students, Research scholars, fiscal analysts and the taxation theorists. I believe that the book will seek to offer a guideline for further intellectual exercises on the same line.

I would like to place on record my deep sense of indebtedness to Prof. T. Mathew, from whom I learnt and developed an interest for Public Finance.

My obligations to all my colleagues in the Department of Economics, NEHU, Shillong, who have been the guiding spirit and the beacon light in all my endeavors, shall remain ever unpaid.

I owe a a special debt of gratitude to Prof. E.D.Thomas, Prof. S.K.Mishra and Prof. P.Nayak and Dr. P.S. Suresh who have helped and encouraged me in various ways while preparing the manuscript.

I find no words to give my innermost feelings for my wife (Sujata) and my son (Echo) for their silent sacrifices without which, I could not have dreamt of completing this work.

I dedicate this humble work to all of teachers who taught me Economics.

B. Mishra

LIST OF TABLES

CHAPTER: I
INTRODUCTION

1.1 Background of the Study

In recent years the government activities vis-à-vis public expenditure have grown both relatively and absolutely in all the states of the Indian federation. With the expansion of the Governmental activities, the magnitude of plan expenditures of the state Governments have increased tremendously which in turn has given rise to the need for a rapid increase in revenue. This has resulted in a situation where, most of the state Governments have increasingly began to restructure their tax system to generate higher revenue or to improve the taxable capacity or tax efforts with a motive to counterbalance the ever increasing public expenditures. Further it is generally felt that to a large extent, the financial problems of the state arise from its lack of tax efforts, i.e. its failure to mobilize adequate resources to meet its increasing demand for various developmental public expenditure programmes. In working out a developmental plan which implicitly takes into account both the tax and public expenditure ratios; a major question that always arises is how much tax and non-tax revenues can a country/ state reasonably expect to raise and what sources should be tapped in order to meet the ever increasing demand for public expenditures so as to bridge up the widening fiscal gap?

In a federal set up, the financing of the state development plans depends to a great extent on the mobilization of resources by the state Governments mainly through the imposition of varieties of taxation. Efforts made in this direction from time to time have not uniformly succeeded. Being federal in structure, the state Governments has limited statutory powers to levy taxes to finance its various infrastructural facilities and welfare programmes. This may be ascribed to the fact that while bulk of the federal revenue has been derived from more elastic sources, implying that the revenue from these taxes increases proportionately, if not faster than income, the sources of the state Government are relatively less elastic, as reported by Rao (1992)[1].

Further, in the recent past, the Federal Government has signaled a general resource crunch. This has necessitated reduction on outlays on the centrally sponsored development schemes to the states on the one hand and a major cut in subsidies and grants on the other. Thus, the outlays of the states have been substantially affected, thereby forcing the State Governments to postpone some of their developmental programmes. This has no doubt slowed down the pace of economic development of the states. As a result the existing pattern of resource allocation of the financial resources between the union of India and its constituent units has generated imbalances between the revenue capacities and the needs of the states much to the disadvantage of the backward states and particularly the states in north-eastern India. In this context, the present study is a humble attempt to enquire into the nature, causes and dimensions of such maladjustments and imbalances in different states in North-Eastern Region.

With the expansion of the Governmental activities, the magnitude of plan expenditures of the state Governments have increased tremendously which in turn has given rise to the need for a rapid increase in revenue. It is expected that, the sources of revenue should grow automatically at the required rate. But the experiences of most of the state Governments in India negate the above proposition. As a result of which, this has created a widening gap between the state's expenditure responsibilities on the one hand and available resources on the other, thereby giving rise to the problem of attaining an appropriate degree of financial self-reliance on the part of the most of the state Governments in India. However it is also felt that to a large extent, the financial problems of the states arise owing to lack of tax efforts on their own part to raise additional resources. On this account, the need for an in-depth analysis of the fiscal anomalies at the state level has been felt for quite some time.

In federal India, the emergence of a situation is evident in which, some states are excessively dependent on federal transfers, while others resort extensively to overdrafts, which can be attributed either to the failure on the part of the state Governments in tapping all the productive sources of revenue or to the fact that a 'critical limit' as regards to tax effort as well as taxable capacity has already reached in case of most the states. This excessive dependence of the states on the centre is not all conducive to the development of sound federal fiscal conventions. This scenario makes a strong case for analyzing the states fiscal condition.

Thus the existing pattern of resource allocation of the financial resources between the union of India and its constituent units has generated imbalances between the revenue capacities and the needs of the States much to the disadvantage of the backward states of India. In this particular context, we have made a successful attempt at enquiring into the nature, causes and dimensions of such maladjustments and imbalances, taking North-Eastern Regions as typically backward states.

To counter balance this, it is believed , that the State Governments may have to resort to either of the following two alternatives to seek higher revenue.

(i) The first recourse before the State Governments may be to re-structure their tax system in such a way so as to yield more revenue. But, the manner in which increasing revenue may be realized through a properly structured tax system at any given time is largely conditioned not only by the various socio-economic and political factors, but also by the efficiency of the State's administrative apparatus, which sets important limits to the ambit, pattern and structure of taxation (Lakdawala, D. T. and Nambiar, K. V., 1972)[2]. We must make absolutely clear at the outset that, there has been no attempt on our part to go into this particular aspect of the problem.

(ii) The second alternative that we can spell out runs in terms of improving the revenue elasticity and buoyancy of the tax structure, so that the tax system will show an automatic response to the growth of the Net State's Domestic Product. The high degree of tax responsiveness to our view may set a limit to an 'optimal level' of taxation on the one hand and to an 'optimal level' of tax effort on the other. To what extent, the State's Government can achieve or have already achieved this objective is an open question. Therefore, the present study is a modest effort in this direction to find out a suitable answer to the above question, by taking into account this second aspect of the problem of State's finances.

1.2 Problem Formulation

Over a period of time, North-Eastern states have developed a dependency syndrome as it is evident from an explosive cycle of public expenditure growth in most of the states of the region, coupled with an increasing demand for grants-in-aids and other Central assistance to bridge the gap of large budgetary deficits. The inadequacy in generating their own sources of revenue to meet the challenge of a volatile fiscal situation may be attributed to a number of factors. They are : (i) the low level of economic activities coupled with a low level of economic base, which may be considered as a product of low level of infrastructural development (ii) emergence of a parallel economy not only due to flourishing trade of imported goods and commodities from the neighboring countries but also due to the various fringe tax benefits of direct taxation particularly of Income tax and lastly (iii) due to the social unrest and political instability that these economies experience from time to time. As a whole, the repercussion effects of all these forces at work has resulted in various leakages not only in tax generating capacity but also in narrowing down the tax base of various taxes in the region. If we are to assign a cause- effect relationship to this type of vexed problem then we can argue that the failures on the part of the state governments in this region to mobilize adequate financial resources in order to carry out their various developmental plan programs, has been mainly responsible for their low level of economic activities, low level of economic base and their final culmination in the form of social unrest.

It is evident from the above discussion that most of the State Governments in Indian Federation face severe budgetary pressures with rising demand for expenditures. Further, it is generally argued that the financial problems of the States arise from their lack of tax efforts, i.e., their failure to mobilize adequate resources from sources within their own jurisdiction. As a result of which, the financial dependence of the States on the Union Government has been on the increase in recent years. However, it is felt that, the resources available to the States under present dispensation are not adequate for meeting their requirements. We intend to accomplish this by analyzing fiscal position of Northeastern states from the angles of resource mobilisation (level of revenue) and its utilization (level of public expenditure)

North-Eastern region is comparatively a background

region, where agriculture is the predominant sector, providing means of livelihood to more than 85 percent of the population. Though significant development has taken place in some sphere since Independence, access to opportunities for a 'reasonably minimum' standard of living in this region is one of the lowest in the country. The fiscal health of the states in this region is by no means encouraging at all, where the States' Own Tax Revenue contributes hardly 17 percent of the total tax receipts of the states. Further, the tax revenue constitutes near about 13 percent of the aggregate revenue of the states. In these states, where the states' own tax revenue contributes no more than 10 percent of the state's income and the aggregate Government expenditures constitutes about 115 percent of the state's income. If, we are allowed to use a terminology for this poor state of fiscal affairs, then we will call it a *tribal fiscal dilemma* that haunts all the north-eastern states. In a welfare characterized state, fulfillment of social desire to have a better quality of life is dependent not only on the capacity of the government to mobilize adequate resources but also on the degree of momentum of the economic activities that a state in question attains. In the absence of a desired level of economic tolerance to the expanded economic activities, mobilizations of adequate resources for carrying out their developmental works are left to the mercy of taxable capacity of the states. It is against this back ground, we intend to undertake an inter-temporal study on the efficiency of the tax system in various states in the North Eastern Region. It is, therefore, worthwhile to study the various aspects of the effects of state taxation and expenditures and the dimensions of its movements over the years.

Thus, the overall picture that emerges is that, the tax generating capacity of the North-Eastern states does not cope up with its increased public expenditure programmes, for achieving a desirable rate of economic progress. This exhibits clearly the low level of tax effort measures on the part of the state governments in the overall scheme of resource mobilization for developmental purposes. As a result of which, economic backwardness has been the resultant outcome.

Based on the above logic, it can be argued that if North-Eastern states' tax policy is to serve the ends of economic development, it should aim to attain at least two objectives[3]. One of the most powerful instruments of resource mobilization is considered to be the tax system. Therefore, the tax system should aim at (I) in siphoning off into the state exchequer as much revenues as can be gathered in the tax net (without discouraging the incentives for private savings and investment) and (ii) in helping to release resources for private (or public) investment by reducing current consumption.

In the back drop of the above facts, the study argues that the remedial approach to tackle the ever increasing fiscal gap lies in attaining an appropriate degree of financial self-reliance. No doubt, any attempt by the state governments to achieve financial self reliance will depend upon a sound fiscal capacity. Further, a sound fiscal capacity of a state remains the logical off-shoot of a highly productive, responsive and efficient tax structure. To what extent North-Eastern states' tax system adheres to the notion of sound fiscal capacity remains an open question. Therefore, the two major research questions that we have touched upon in this context are: (i) to measure the extent to which the revenue capacity of these states' tax system has been realized and (ii) to assess the overall success of government measures to increase revenue potentialities of the tax system and the North-Eastern states' overall capacities to raise the tax-income ratio overtime.

There are six available indicators to assess North-Eastern states' performance with respect to the above two objectives. These indicators are: buoyancy and elasticity, compound growth rate, marginal tax rate, tax ratio and tax effort of the tax system in vogue. Of these six indicators, the tax ratio and the tax effort measures generally do not indicate the efficacy of the revenue structure of the states' government as they do not take into account the taxable capacity. Thus, we are left with the choice of applying the compound growth rate and marginal tax rates and elasticity and buoyancy coefficients to the tax structure so as to assess directly the productivity, efficiency and responsiveness of states' tax structure. So, it is clear that, if the state's tax structure satisfies four conditions, namely, that: (i) the marginal tax rate increases with every increase in per capita income; (ii) average tax rate responds positively to the changes in tax base, (iii) the buoyancy of taxes is substantially higher than unity; and (iv) the elasticity is equal to or marginally greater than unity, then it can be said that the states tax system/ resource mobilization prgrammes have performed satisfactorily, given its relative taxable capacity. The effectiveness of North-Eastern states' tax system is assessed in the context of these four norms.

On the state level, tax revenue may change through automatic response of the tax yield to changes in State Income and, or, through the imposition of new taxes, revision of the rates, stricter tax compliance and other administrative measures backed by legal action. Changes in the tax yield resulting from modifying such tax parameters (i.e., rates, bases etc.) are called discretionary changes, which may incidentally involve some legislative action. Changes in the tax yield flowing from the combined effects of automatic responses as well as discretionary changes constitute the "buoyancy" of a tax. On the other hand, with tax parameters held constant (i.e., discretionary changes being removed) automatic changes in the tax yield resulting from variations in the state income measures the "elasticity" of a tax or a tax system.

The need for undertaking such an analysis for the state taxation in North-Eastern States arises due to the following reasons.

Since the buoyancy coefficient compares the actual growth of tax revenue with the growth in State Income, it indicates the following resultant outcome. First, it helps in assessing the overall success of Government's measures to increase tax revenue. Secondly, to the extent that the buoyancy is low, it would suggest a need for devising a tax structure which would overcome the deficiencies. Thirdly, on the basis of such study, the state Government can estimate the probable tax revenue with unchanged base and the rate of tax, consequent on more increase in the State Income.

The elasticity coefficient on the other hand, indicates the inherent responsiveness of a tax system to changes in the State Income and also it reflects, how far the revenue potential of a given tax system has been realized.

It is against this theoretical problem, a humble attempt is being made in this work, to throw some light on the problems of estimating elasticity and buoyancy of the state taxes in the North-Eastern Region, in order to determine the degree of responsiveness of the state taxes to the state's Domestic Product. This is to our view will exhibit the relative degree of efficiency of state tax measures and will indicate the extent of additional tax efforts needed to increase the revenue of the Government.

1.3 Scope and Objectives of the Study

The study covered a period of 38 years from 1963 to 2001. This is a period during which the North-Eastern States' economy has passed through phases of both upswing and downswing owing to wide fluctuations in their agricultural sector as well as political instability and social tensions. Further, this entire period witnessed political instability and social tensions leading to substantial changes both in its expenditure and taxation policies in the entire North-eastern States. It may be mentioned here that the relevant data on discretionary changes in tax revenue are unavailable for the states of Mizoram, Tripura, Manipur and Arunachal Pradesh.

Therefore, for the purpose of inter state comparison of the elasticity and buoyancy coefficients within the North-Eastern region; we made an attempt to estimate the discretionary response of the various taxes of these states by taking into account the tax base of various taxes and the the changes in tax rates over the years. To that extent, the tax responsiveness analysis of these states may slightly over state or under state the results. It may be mentioned that wherever possible, for the inter-state comparison within the North-Eastern region, we thought it imperative to take two representative states, namely Meghalaya and Nagaland as the area of our study. The reason for choosing these two states is one fold. It is observed that in recent years, the state of Meghalaya has preferred to maintain a surplus budget while that of the state of Nagaland continues to have a deficit budget over the years. Thus, we believe that inter state comparison between these two representative states may throw some light on the scope of additional resource mobilisation and the resultant patterns of its utilization in other different states of North-Eastern region. Keeping these general problems in view, an attempt has been made in this work to study in detail the following aspects of state taxes.

(i) An assessment of the overall success of the Government measures to increase Government revenue.

(ii) An analysis of the growth of tax revenue consequent on the growth of Gross State Domestic Product and, to determine the extent to which the North-eastern region's tax system is responsive to changes in State Income overtime.

(iii) To measure the extent to which the revenue potential of the North-eastern region's tax system has been realized.

However, the main focus of our study as mentioned earlier has been on the analysis of elasticity and buoyancy of the tax system as a whole and of each individual tax to changes in tax base and in the State Income.

1.4. Sources and Limitation of Data

The study has been based primarily on the secondary sources of data. The main sources of data are; Annual budgets/ Finance account of the various state governments including their memorandum submitted to the various finance commissions for the period covered by our study. Whenever possible, the budgetary data relating to India published in CMIE and RBI annual reports on Currency and Finance were used and consulted. We have also used wherever possible the budgetary data relating to India as published from time to time in the Reserve Bank Bulletin and the RBI annual reports on Currency and Finance.

1.5 Methodology

The data has been analyzed with the help of suitable statistical techniques and the results obtained have been subjected to relevant economic logic.

Simple regression equations are fitted to the data (by the method of least square) to estimate the trends and fluctuations in revenues and expenditures of the two representative states of North-Eastern region for the period under study. To study the shifts in the relative shares of various taxes and non-tax sources in states' own revenue, we have made use of the statistical technique of time series analysis. Specific techniques and measures are described fully as and when used.

1.6. Work Plan

The topical organization of the work is as follows. For the purpose of expositional convenience and systematic analysis, the work has been divided into six parts namely (1) Introduction, (2) Review of Literature and Methodology (3) problems and prospects of resource mobilisation of the states (4) Expenditure policies of the states (5)Elasticity and buoyancy of state tax system as a whole and that of individual taxes, and (6) Policy Implications.

Chapter -1 is intended to be Introductory in nature. In this section, we have addressed ourselves to the intricate problems and issues involved in the state finance. Besides, this chapter also incorporates a description of the methodology followed in this study and the sources and limitations of data.

Chapter-II is devoted to the statistical methods used to evaluate the fiscal position of the North-Eastern states. An attempt has been made to give a comprehensive account of the major conceptual and empirical issues relating to the analysis of tax efforts and tax responsiveness. An attempt is made to develop an alternative model of elasticity and buoyancy for measuring the responsiveness of North-Eastern Region's tax system by taking into account the difficulties associated with the estimation of elasticity and buoyancy of the tax system.

Chapter - III is an attempt to examine the problems and prospects of financial resources of the states. The purpose of this is to present an over view of all the states' finance for determining the degree of financial dependency of the state on the Union government. An attempt has also been made in this chapter to determine the extent to which North-Eastern region's economy is financially self-reliant in mobilizing adequate resources from sources within its own jurisdiction. An attempt is made in this chapter to apply the first group of indicators as mentioned earlier, i.e. Compound growth rate, Marginal and Average tax rate to asses the level of fiscal tolerance of the region.

Chapter - IV is concerned with the critical analysis of public expenditure growth, where we made an attempt to assess the overall utilization pattern of the states' financial resources for the entire 38 years covered by our study. We have also carried out a brief analysis of the growth of public expenditure consequent upon the growth of Gross State Domestic Product in order to ascertain its degree of variation with respect to states' income. It may be mentioned here that for the purpose of inter state comparison within the North-Eastern region, we thought it imperative to take two representative states, namely Meghalaya and Nagaland to ascertain the intricacies of of public expenditure growth in the North-Eastern States. The reason for choosing these two states is one fold. It is observed that in recent years, the state of Meghalaya has preferred to maintain a surplus budget while that of the state of Nagaland continues to have a deficit budget over the years. Thus, we believe that inter state comparison between these two representative states may throw some light on the resultant patterns of its utilization in other different states of North-Eastern region.

An estimation of elasticity and buoyancy of the state tax system as a whole is carried out in Chapter-V., and, in Chapter -VI, we present the policy implications.

Notes and References

1. Rao, M. G.; "Proposal for State Level Budgetary Reforms", paper presented at IIDs seminar on Fiscal Discipline and Fiscal Consolidation at the central and state level IIDs, Calcutta, February 19, 1992 (mimeo).
2. Lakdawala, D.T. and Nambiar, K.V.,; "Commodity Taxation in India", Ahmedabad, Sardar Patel Institute of Economic and Social Research, 1972, p. 1.
3. Alternative statements of the objectives of development oriented taxation policy discussed in theliterature include :
   (i) The Promotion of Distributive Justice, (T. Barna, Redistribution of income through public Finance, Cxford Claredan Press, 1945); (Richard, M. Bird Public Finance and Inequality, Finance and Development, March, 1947, pp. 2-4).

(ii) The Promotion of Industry; (Robert, B. Bangs, Planning and Economic Development : Fiscal policy for emerging countries, University of Chicago Press, 1968, p. 119).

(iii) The Rationalization of Taxation Structure, (Benjamin Higgins, Economic Development : Principles, Problems and Policies, Central Book Depot, Allahabad, 1966, p. 509).

(iv) The expansion of employment opportunities, (Bird, R. M. and Oldman, O. (eds.), Readings on Taxation in Developing Countries, John Hopkins Press, 1972).

(v) The gradual reduction of reliance on indirect taxes, (Due, John F., Indirect Taxation in Developing Countries, John Hopkins Press, 1970; Government of India, Report of Indirect Taxation Enquiry Committee, part 1, October 1977, p. 2).

(vi) The mobilization of savings or surplus mobilization, (Kaldor, Nicholas; Taxation for Economic Development, Journal of modern African studies, vol. 1, No. 1, 1963, pp. 7-11; Chelliah, Raja J., fiscal policy in underdeveloped countries, George Allen and Unwin (India) Ltd., 1969, p. 66).

CHAPTER– II

METHODOLOGY

2.1 Introduction

This chapter is an attempt to give a detailed note on the statistical methods that are employed in this work to assess the fiscal scenario in the north-Eastern states. As discussed in the previous chapter, it was thought to be imperative to evaluate the efficiency of the fiscal policy measures in the North-Eastern states by applying four indicators such as: compound growth rate, Average and marginal tax rates, buoyancy and elasticity.

2.2 Compound Growth Rates

To analyze the relative growth of different sources of tax and non-tax revenues, exponential growth rates were calculated by using the formula:

$$Y = ae^{rt}$$

Where, Y is the revenue from a particular tax or non-tax source as the case might be and 't' is the time period and 'r' is the growth rate. The least square estimate of the above formula has been worked out to arrive at the exponential growth rate figures.

2.3 Average and Marginal Tax Rates

In order to have a more meaningful analysis of the changing tax-income ratio, we have to relate the Average

Tax Rate with the Marginal Tax Rate. The purpose of relating these two measures of the tax-income ratio is two fold.

First, the concept of marginal rate of taxation is useful in relation to a discussion on the appropriateness of the disposition of additional national income among several uses in any given country[1]. The marginal tax rate determines whether, and how fast, the tax ratio increases in the context of an increase in income over time. It is usually hypothesized that a high marginal tax rate is a product of higher per capita income.

Second, the Average Tax Rate of the base period is likely to influence the marginal rate in so far as it is possible for a given tax system to take out the same fraction from the incremental income as that from the original income base. Further, this will indicate the degree of variations in the tax revenue with respect to changes in the tax base.

The Average Tax rates (ATR) have been calculated using following formula:

ATR = Amount of taxes collected ÷ Size of the taxable base

The formula may be described symbolically as follows:

If, AR_i and PB_i are the actual revenue and the potential base respectively for the ith tax in the state, then, the average tax rate is:

$$ATR_i = \frac{ARi}{PBi}$$

For estimating the Marginal Tax Rate (MTR), the following formula is used.

MTR = Absolute change in Tax Revenue ÷ Absolute change in Tax Base

or, symbolically, we can put it:

$$MTR = \frac{\Delta\ TR}{\Delta\ TB}$$

Where, MTR = Marginal Tax Rate

Δ TR = change in Tax Revenue, and

Δ TB = change in Tax Base.

2.4 Buoyancy and Elasticity

An attempt is also made here, to review the responsiveness and productivity of North-eastern states' tax system in terms of elasticity and buoyancy, to measure the relative degree of efficiency of the state's tax measures on the one hand, and to indicate the extent of additional tax efforts needed to increase the revenue of the government on the other.

On the state level, the changes in tax revenue yield may come about through 'automatic' response of the tax yields to changes in Net State Domestic Product (NSDP) and/or, through the imposition of new taxes, revision of the rate structure of existing taxes, expansion of the tax base, and other administrative measures backed by legal action.

Changes in tax yield resulting from modifying tax parameters (i.e. rate, base, etc.) are called 'discretionary changes'. They are the product of legislative action. With tax parameters held constant (i.e. discretionary) changes being removed), automatic changes in tax yield resulting from variations in NSDP measures the elasticity of a tax system. However changes in the tax yield flowing from the combined effect of 'automatic' changes and 'discretionary' changes are a measure of the 'buoyancy' of a tax or a tax system.

To measure elasticity, it is necessary to separate the effects of changes in tax revenue with respect to "Base". When, T is related to "Income" as well as "Base", the multiple regression model suggested by the empirical analysis in the literature[2],

$$\text{Log T} = a_1 + a_2 \log Y + a_3 \log B + U \quad \text{———————} (1)$$

where, T = Total tax yield,

Y = state income

B = Tax Base, U = disturbance term and,

a_i = estimates of the parameters (i = 0,1,2)

does give the account of tax estimation, where the other variables like tax rate and its growth etc. are not incorporated into the model. On this ground, we thought it imperative to substitute the variable D (as defined earlier) for B, where D includes all sorts of discretionary changes. If, we will have to believe that estimate of tax be separable as automatic response (elasticity) and discretionary response, then, the combination of these two responses, will give us the buoyancy of a tax or that of the tax system as a whole. Then,

$$T = T_D + T_Y \quad \text{———————————} (2)$$

where, T_D = Response of the tax to discretionary changes (B)

T_Y = Automatic response of the tax to changes in income (Y)

and, T = Total unadjusted tax yields from theses two effects.

So, from the total response of the tax (T), we will have to separate the effects' of income and the effects of discretionary changes (base). But, this is not an easy task unless, we know the marginal probability distribution of tax with respect to both automatic as well as discretionary changes.

Since, in the equation (1), the discretionary response and automatic response of the tax are given by the estimates of a_3 and a_2 (being a log-linear model) and these are constant throughout the period under study, it would be mathematically possible to estimate that part of tax revenue which will be accounted only by automatic response (Income) or discretionary response (Base), e.g., the empirical equation:

$$\text{Log } \hat{T} = \hat{a}1 + \hat{a}2 \log Y + \hat{a}3 \log D \quad \text{——————} (3)$$

from which, after taking anti-log, we can get the adjusted tax revenue series as

$$T - \theta_1 T \approx Ta \qquad (4)$$

where, $\theta_1 T = \hat{a}_3 \log D$ (i.e. the response of the tax to the discretionary measures).

Then, we can re-estimate,

$$Ta = a_4 + a_5 \log Y \qquad (5)$$

The above equation will give us the elasticity. In this process, we eliminated the effect of discretionary changes from the original multiple regression. The same procedures could be used also for eliminating the effect of income from the tax by subtracting from,

$$T - \theta_2 T = T_D \qquad (6)$$

where, T_D =Response of the tax due to discretionary measures.

The theoretical considerations though appear to be sound, but due to the presence of constant (intercept), when both Discretionary and income variables act as independent variables then, this constant term of the empirical equation may be partly influenced by income and partly by the discretionary variable in an indirect way, or, it may be free from their effect. According to empiricists, tax could only be a function of both Y and D, or, Y and D separately. That means, the contribution of Y and D, both separately and as well as jointly can be seen from the model structure. But, then the constant term α_0-how could we explain! Therefore, we may suggest a regression equation, which is going through the mean value of the variables, then, we can avoid the problem of α_0. For example,

$$\log(T - \overline{T}) = \hat{\alpha}_1 \log(Y - \overline{Y}) + \hat{\alpha}_2 \log(D - \overline{D}) \qquad (7)$$

Where, $\overline{T}, \overline{Y}, \overline{D}$ are the mean values of T, Y, and D respectively. We may also think that α_0 is free from the effect of both Y and D. This contribution to the tax given by the value of α_0 are those functions such as additional tax efforts, new means adopted for resource mobilisation etc., which are always inherent in the tax structure. That is why, when we are estimating T relating to Y or, T relating to D alone we used,

$$T = \theta_1 T - (D) \quad \text{———} \quad (8)$$

$$T = \theta_2 T - (Y) \quad \text{———} \quad (9)$$

Where, $\theta_1 = \hat{a}_3 \log D$, and, $\theta_2 = \hat{a}_4 \log Y$.

Therefore, we have to make an alternative way of removing the effect of either the discretionary factor or the income factor. For example, we take,

$$\text{Log } T = a_6 + a_7 \log Y + U \quad \text{———} \quad (10)$$

Here, the assumption is that the total tax is explained by income alone. The empirical equation,

$$\text{Log } \hat{T} = \hat{a}_6 + \hat{a}_7 \log Y \quad \text{———} \quad (11)$$

gives the estimate of tax as a function of income. Here, the intercept term gives the account of that element of tax which is beyond the ambit of the model, say, extraneous causes, but certainly not by income variable. We estimate,

$$T_d = T - Ty \quad \text{———} \quad (12)$$

$$\text{Now,} \quad Ty \approx \theta_3 \approx a_6 \log Y \quad \text{———} \quad (13)$$

if, our assumptions are correct then, we re-estimate,

$$T_d = \hat{a}_8 + \hat{a}_9 \log D \quad \text{———} \quad (14)$$

Though, $\hat{a}_8$ still present in the model, this is bound to be smaller than $\hat{a}_{10}$ of,

$$\text{Log } \hat{T} = \hat{a}_{10} + \hat{a}_{11} \log D \quad \text{———} \quad (15)$$

This is not only probability, but, the empirical evidence will support the view.

We have to consider one fact that in the previous chapters, we have been discussing the variations of tax realizations in different years, which have to be also supported by empirical evidence within the model. For this reason, we may suggest a linear equation as against the log linear equation. In a multiplicative type of the model, the total effect of any change does not conform to the theory of additivity. For example,

$$Y = a + bx \quad \text{——————} \quad (16)$$

and, $$\text{Log } Y = \log a + b \log x \quad \text{——————} \quad (17)$$

where, Y denotes tax revenue

x denotes Net State Domestic Product

and, b denotes regression coefficient.

Here, a + b of the equation (16) = 1. But, in the log linear equation, represented by equation (17), $a + b \neq 1$. For the simple reason, to explain the variation of tax for every single year, we would prefer a linear equation, which supports the additivity property of the parameters estimates.

Next, we have to consider another theoretical constraint. The authorities investigating the buoyancy and elasticity of tax revenue have adopted with solid grounding that,

$$T = f_1 (Y)$$
$$T = f_2 (D) \quad \text{——————} \quad (18)$$
$$D = f_3 (Y)$$

This would lead us to the problem of multicollinearity. In that case, the model will be,

$$\text{Log } T = a + b \log Y + c \log B + U \text{——————} (19)$$

This is inconsistent and untenable econometrically. Therefore, we have to make a compromise by adopting only the 2-variables model suggested by these functions.

Further, we know that we rely on the independent Variables to such an extent that at least 50 percent of the total variability could be explained. The coefficient of determination (R^2) will tell us this. But, often from practice, we find that any addition of independent variables will contribute to R^2 but at the cost of reliability of the estimates of the parameters. Also, in time series type of analysis, the disturbance term 'U' does not behave in the way we expect, as often, there is serial correlation of the disturbance term. If, we consider the 1st order auto-regression function of the disturbance term, then, we can express,

$$U_t = \rho U_{t-1} + V_t \quad \text{———} (20)$$

and, the estimate of ρ can be obtained by:

$$\rho = \frac{\Sigma U_t U_{t-1}}{\Sigma U_{t-1}^2} \quad \text{———} (21)$$

Keeping this in mind, that P is also affecting the reliability of the estimate, we re-introduce the earlier model as such,

$$\text{Log } T_t = a_{1t} + a_{2t} \log Y_t + a_{3t} \log D_t + U_t \quad \text{———} (22)$$

and, with one period log,

$$\text{Log } T_{t-1} = a_{1t-1} + a_{2t-1} \log Y_{t-1} + a_{3t-1} \log D_{t-1} + U_{t-1} \quad \text{———} (23)$$

Multiplying the lagged equation by ρ throughout and subtracting from the 1st, we obtain,

$$(\text{Log } T_t - \rho T_t) = (a_{1t} - \rho_{a1t-1}) + (a_{2t} - \rho a_{2t-1})$$
$$\text{Log } (Y_t - PY_{t-1}) + (a_{3-1} - \rho a_{3t-1})$$
$$\text{Log } (B_t - \rho D_{t-1}) + (U_t - \rho U_{t-1}) \quad \text{———} (24)$$

if, we express the above equation (24) as,

$$\text{Log } Tt^* = a_{1t}^* + a_{2t}^* \log Yt^* + a_{3t}^* \log D_t^* + V_t^* \quad \text{———} (25)$$

Then,this V_t^* will have to hold the same properties as the U_t.

If, we now follow the same procedure in isolating "income" or "discretionary" effect, then we can estimate the automatic response and the discretionary response that constitute the total tax revenue.

In conclusion, for our analysis, we may adopt the following models.

$$T = a_0 + a_1 Y + U_1 \quad \text{———} (26)$$

$$TA = a_2 + a_3Y + U_2 \quad \text{————} \quad (27)$$

$$T = a_4 + a_5Y + a_6D + U_3 \quad \text{————} \quad (28)$$

where, T = Actual tax revenue realized

TA = Adjusted tax revenue after taking out discretionary effects.

D = Discretionary effort of tax realization.

U_i = Stochastic disturbance term.

and, Y = state income.

Equation (26) measures the buoyancy of tax revenue, whereas equation (27) measures the elasticity of tax revenue we may also adopt log linear version of the above models. Equation (28) measures the total responsiveness of the tax or the tax system, which is decomposed into two effects namely income response and discretionary response.

Notes and References

1. Chelliah, Raja J. - Trends in Taxation in Developing countries, in Richard M. Bird and Oliver Oldman (edt.), "Readings on Taxation in Developing Countries", London, The Johns Hopkins University Press, 1975, p. 109.

   Auld, D.A.L. (1971), "Automatic Fiscal Stabilizers: Problems of Identification and Measurement", *Journal of Public Finance*, Vol. 26, No. 4, pp.513-31.

2. Rao, V.G., The Responsiveness of the Indian Tax System 1960-61 to 1973-74, Banglore, Allied Publishers Pvt. Ltd. (1970).

CHAPTER- III

PROBLEMS AND PROSPECTS OF INTERNAL RESOURCE MOBILISATION

3.1. Introduction

In the preceding chapters, it has been pointed out that the main cause of a explosive cycle of expenditure growth in the North-eastern region is the continuous outpacing of the growth of public expenditure to the growth public revenue. This has necessitated the state governments to increase its tax revenues to a considerable extent. The willingness and capacity of the government to respond to this need has been an important determinant to its capacity to carry forward developmental plan programmes. However, in the absence of any consistent long-term policy objectives accompanied by non-significant structural changes and the absence of flexibility and adaptability in these economies, the resource problem has remained a measure policy issue.

3.2 Thrust of the Problem

Therefore, an attempt is made in this chapter to examine the problem of resource constraint and prospects of internal resource mobilization in the state during the last thirty-eight years of planning covered by the study. It may be mentioned here that the revenue constraints and the problem of resource mobilization are explained in terms of existing contribution

: different taxes by reflecting their share in the Net State ·omestic Product (NSDP) and compositional structural ıaracter of different taxes on the basis of ratios and trends s well.

.3 Problem of Internal Resource Mobilization

In the following paragraph, an attempt is made to ·xamine the trends in the revenue yields from different taxes ınd also their relative place in the system of taxation.

It is intended to study the composition of tax revenues or the relative importance of the specified individual taxes in the tax system in terms of either the percentage of different taxes in total tax revenue or the ratio of these taxes to Net State Domestic Product as these two aspects of changes are inter related. It is believed that an enquiry of this nature besides throwing some light on the underlining forces at work would be found useful in evaluating actual and potential performances of the state governments in the matter of resource mobilization.

3.4 Feasible Trends in Tax Effort

Before going into the details of the individual tax items of the state and the Union (shared taxes), an examination of their combined yields vis-à-vis state income is essential, because these give an overall idea about the extent to which the state government has been able to mobilise additional resources into the public sector savings. This, no doubt, will exhibit the relative tax effort of the government. Table 3.1(a) and 3.1(b) facilitate such an analysis for the state of Nagaland and Meghalaya respectively.

Column 1 of both the tables indicates the State's Own Tax revenue. This shows that during the span of thirty-eight years plan period, State's Own Tax revenue in case of Nagaland has increased in absolute terms, roughly one hundred and thirty one fold, from Rs.0.6 crores in 1963-64 to Rs.79.00 crores in 2000-01 where as in case of Meghalaya,

State's own tax revenue has increased in absolute terms more than a hundred and sixteen fold, from Rs. 1.21 crores in 1972-73 to Rs. 140.45 crores in 2001-02. Thus the growth rates of the own tax revenue in both the states follows more or less the similar pattern and magnitude. This increase of State's Own Tax revenue over the years was mainly due to large receipts under Sales Tax, state Excise Duty, Professional Tax and tax on income and expenditures, all of which have increased considerably over these years. The increase in absolute terms of these taxes may be attributed to the extension of tax base and tax coverage of these taxes and also due to an upward revision of the tax rates during these years. Further, an upward trend in the growth of State Domestic product might have contributed to the observed tread to certain extent

Table 3.1(a): Tax Revenue and State Income of Nagaland, 1963-64 to 2000-2001

(Rs.in crores)

0	1	2	3	4	5	6
Year	State's Own Tax Revenue	Total Tax Revenue	State Income	As a % of Col.1 to Col.3	As a % of Col.1 to Col.3	Ratio of Col.1 to Col.2
1963-64	0.06	0.09	5.90	1.00	1.50	0.66
1964-65	0.24	0.32	8.70	2.70	3.60	0.75
1965-66	0.32	0.44	13.80	2.30	3.10	0.72
1966-67	0.26	0.42	16.10	1.60	2.60	0.61
1967-68	0.35	0.52	18.40	1.90	2.80	0.67
1968-69	0.33	0.55	20.90	1.50	2.60	0.60
1969-70	0.46	0.71	22.10	2.00	3.20	0.64
1970-71	0.61	0.93	24.80	2.40	3.70	0.65
1971-72	0.75	1.05	28.30	2.60	3.80	0.68
1972-73	1.36	1.73	35.60	3.80	4.80	0.78

(Contd...)

0	1	2	3	4	5	6
1973-74	1.94	2.41	41.50	4.60	5.80	0.80
1974-75	1.93	2.69	49.20	3.90	5.40	0.71
1975-76	2.86	3.75	56.70	5.00	6.60	0.76
1976-77	5.59	3.64	63.90	4.00	5.60	0.71
1977-78	2.87	4.00	73.20	3.90	5.40	0.71
1978-79	3.35	4.62	86.60	3.80	5.30	0.72
1979-80	4.19	6.58	109.20	3.30	6.00	0.63
1980-81	5.19	7.83	132.30	3.90	5.90	0.66
1981-82	6.36	9.45	163.30	3.80	5.70	0.67
1982-83	7.45	10.79	207.50	3.50	5.20	0.69
1983-84	10.46	14.34	255.10	4.10	5.60	0.72
1984-85	12.46	16.72	231.40	5.30	7.20	0.74
1985-86	15.39	80.51	261.10	5.80	30.83	0.19
1986-87	15.69	86.46	293.90	4.60	29.00	0.18
1987-88	20.25	105.74	337.90	6.00	31.00	0.90
1988-89	19.49	130.79	361.20	5.30	36.20	0.14
1989-90	17.44	93.78	432.90	4.00	21.60	0.18
1990-91	18.64	138.46	662.50	2.80	20.80	0.13
1991-92	21.61	161.50	761.50	2.80	21.20	0.13
1992-93	19.75	186.87	841.50	2.30	22.20	0.10
1993-94	25.08	192.05	879.50	2.80	21.80	0.13
1994-95	25.72	213.23	1258.70	2.00	16.90	0.12
1995-96	43.28	209.33	1655.90	2.60	12.60	0.20
1996-97	57.06	307.30	1848.50	3.00	16.60	0.18
1997-98	71.07	452.03	2136.80	3.30	21.10	0.15
1998-99	61.96	472.91	2183.82	2.80	21.60	0.13
1999-00	71.04	548.06	-	-	-	0.12
2000-01	79.00	620.94	-	-	-	0.12

Sources:Government of Nagaland, Finance Account (1963-64 to 1997-98; Statistical Abstract of Nagaland, 1966, 1975, 1990, 2000; Estimate of Net State Domestic Product 2000.

Table 3.1 (b) Tax Revenue and State Income of Meghalaya (1972-73 to 2001-2002)
(Rs.in crores)

0	1	2	3	4	5	6
Year	State's Own Tax	Total Tax Revenue	State Income	Col. 1 as a % of	Col.2 as a % Col.1 to	Col. 1 as a % Col.2
1972-73	1.21	3.33	105.09	1.15	3.17	0.36
1973-74	1.55	3.86	108.36	1.43	3.56	0.40
1974-75	1.95	4.18	111.97	1.74	3.73	0.47
1975-76	2.18	5.10	115.51	1.89	4.42	0.43
1976-77	2.48	5.57	120.08	2.07	4.64	0.45
1977-78	2.58	5.82	134.75	1.91	4.32	0.44
1978-79	3.39	6.97	149.77	2.26	4.65	0.49
1979-80	4.04	10.56	165.46	2.44	6.38	0.38
1980-81	4.88	12.07	179.62	2.72	6.72	0.40
1981-82	6.20	14.23	205.84	3.01	6.91	0.44
1982-83	7.37	16.09	227.10	3.25	7.08	0.46
1983-84	9.50	19.36	263.14	3.61	7.36	0.49
1984-85	12.24	22.91	302.27	4.05	7.58	0.53
1985-86	14.93	60.45	341.53	4.37	17.70	0.25
1986-87	17.74	73.00	386.25	4.59	18.90	0.24
1987-88	19.61	84.91	466.86	4.20	18.19	0.23

(Contd...)

0	1	2	3	4	5	6
1988-89	27.72	110.19	505.96	5.48	21.78	0.25
1989-90	32.26	97.52	659.78	4.88	14.78	0.33
1990-91	36.01	116.37	767.35	4.69	15.17	0.31
1991-92	42.54	147.81	884.22	4.81	16.72	0.29
1992-93	44.18	169.82	978.54	4.51	17.35	0.26
1993-94	47.93	175.75	1133.38	4.23	15.51	0.27
1994-95	56.27	200.90	1258.04	4.47	15.97	0.28
1995-96	66.26	225.97	1380.31	4.80	16.37	0.29
1996-97	77.37	294.94	1485.28	5.21	19.86	0.26
1997-98	73.55	360.32	1690.42	4.35	21.32	0.20
1998-99	88.36	388.91	2079.25	4.25	18.70	0.23
1999-00	102.98	444.74	2467.13	4.17	18.03	0.23
2000-01	132.48®	296.73	2806.20	4.72	10.57	0.45
2001-02	140.45©	323.61	3267.36	4.30	9.90	0.43

Source: Budget in Brief, Government of Meghalaya: 1974-75; 1977-78; 1978-79; 1982-83; 1983-84

Budget at a Glance, Government of Meghalaya: 1984-85; 1989-90; 1994-95; 1996-97; 1998-99; 2001-02

Estimates of State Domestic Product of Meghalaya, 1980-81 to 1995-96, Government of Meghalaya, Directorate of Economics and Statistics, Meghalaya, Shillong,

State Economy, Government of Meghalaya, Directorate of Economics and Statistics

*Note: Net State Domestic Product figures are in current prices.

® = Revised Estimate

© = Budget Estimate

Column 2 of the Table exhibits the trend of total tax revenue of the States during the period covered by the study. It is to be noted that the annual compound rate of growth of total tax revenue during the period under consideration was approximately 38.89 and 18.59 per cent for the states of Nagaland and Meghalaya respectively.

Further the tables indicate a rising trend of the total tax revenue over the years for both the states. Since the total tax revenue includes shared taxes, the higher exponential growth rate may be ascribed to the better tax mobilization efforts made by the Central Government from time to time. Further, higher growth of total taxes in Nagaland's situation indicates the degree of elasticity and buoyancy that are inherent in the shared taxes resulting in a larger devolution of resources from the Centre to the State by way of higher share in the Central taxes.

The data presented in column 3 of the above tables is the aggregate of the sector-wise estimates by industrial origin of the State Domestic Product at factor cost at current prices. Although the state Domestic Product in both these two states had increased in absolute terms, the exponential growth rates gives some distressing results.

If, we express the relationship between the tax revenues and state income in the usual tax-income ratio terms, Table 1.1.1(a) and (b) reveal some interesting results.

Column 4 of the same Tables presents the percentage of State's own tax revenue to the net state domestic product over the years. The percentage of State's own tax revenue to net state domestic product in the state of Meghalaya, which was 1.15 per cent in 1972-73, increased slowly over the years and stood at 4.30 per cent in 2001-02. Similarly, in Nagaland's situation, the percentage of own tax revenue to net state domestic product has almost remained comparatively static over the years. If, we judge the performances of the State's own tax revenue on the basis of its contribution to the net state domestic product, then the performances of the State's own tax revenue in both the states present a poor picture altogether. The observed trend indicate the failures of both the state governments in mobilising adequate resources from its own taxation measures.

In column 5, is shown the percentage of total tax revenue to the state income. This reveals a continuous increase in percentage share of total tax revenue in the state income over the years in both the states. This shows that over the years, a sizeable share in incremental income has been transferred to the public exchequer.

Column 6 of the above tables shows the ratio of the State's Own Tax revenue to the total tax revenues at accruing to the states during these years. A distressing feature in Naglannd's situation is that the ratio, which was 0.66 in the year 1963-64, has decreased to 0.12 in the year 2000-01. This decreasing ratio of State's Own Tax revenue to state's total tax revenue would seem to indicate that the state has not put in greater efforts than before in raising its own tax revenue in much more conscious way during the period from 1985-86 to 2000-01 and has not tapped more resources from its expanded economic activities thereby not increasing the avenues for financing its own expenditure. Meghalay's experience to this effect is no way different to the observed trend in the state of Nagaland. Table3.1 (b) shows that the ratio which was 0.36 in the year 1972-73 remained more or less stagnant over the years with the ratio of 0.43 in the year 2001-02. The stagnant ratio of the State's own tax revenue to the State's total tax revenue during the period of the study indicates that the State has not put in extra efforts with the passage of time in raising its own tax revenue in a much more efficient way and also has not made any sincere effort to tap more resources.

The compound growth rates were worked out using the

exponential function of the type:

$$Y = ae^{rt}$$

Where, t = tome, Y= the dependent variable and r = growth rate.

Column 1 of the table 3.2. indicates the State's Own Tax revenue. Considered from the point of view of the familiar growth rate, Nagaland's Own Tax revenue has registered a growth rate of 16.92 per cent per annum over the years. Similarly, the growth rate of own tax revenue for Meghalaya has registered a growth rate of 16.71 per cent per annum during the period of our study. Thus the growth rates of the own tax revenue in almost all the states except the state of Arunachal Pradesh follows more or less the similar pattern and magnitude. This increase of State's Own Tax revenue over the years was mainly due to large receipts under Sales Tax, state Excise Duty, Professional Tax and tax on income and expenditures, all of which have increased considerably over these years. The increase in absolute terms of these taxes may be attributed to the extension of tax base and tax coverage of these taxes and also due to an upward revision of the tax rates during these years. The growth rate trend observed in case of shared taxes in all the states indicates that the North-Eastern States have failed miserably in according a reasonable degree of tax responsiveness in terms of the productivity and efficiency to their tax system in comparison to the shared taxes whose growth rates surpass the State's own tax growth rate.

Column 2 of the Table exhibits the trend of total tax revenue of the States during the period covered by our study. It is to be noted that the annual compound rate of growth of total tax revenue during the period under consideration was approximately 38.89 and 18.59 per cent for the states of Nagaland and Meghalaya respectively. Further, the growth of total tax revenue except for the state of Arunachal Pradesh followed more or less the similar pattern.

The table below indicates a rising trend of the total tax revenue over the years for both the states. Since the total tax revenue includes shared taxes, the higher exponential growth rate may be ascribed to the better tax mobilization efforts made by the Central Government from time to time.

Table 3.2.: Compound growth rates of states' own taxes, total taxes and state income

States	Growth of own Tax Revenue	Growth of total tax revenue	State Income
Nagaland	$18.5707 + e^{.16927t}$ $R^2 = 0.9621$	$228.606 + e^{.3883t}$ $R^2 = 0.1789$	$2025.308 + e^{0.038t}$ $R^2 = 0.1427$
Meghalaya	$0.1711 + e^{0.1671t}$ $R^2 = 0.9882$	$0.9657 + e^{0.1859t}$ $R^2 = 0.9628$	$23.7504 + e^{0.1468t}$, $R^2 = 0.9851$
Assam	$0.8675 + e^{0.16845t}$ $R^2 = 0.9356$	$112.341 + e^{0.1926t}$ $R^2 = 0.8569$	$19.8395 + e^{0.1579t}$ $R^2 = 0.9206$
Mizoram	$5.6724 + e^{0.14357t}$ $R^2 = 0.7893$	$56.3954 + e^{0.1748t}$ $R^2 = 0.8694$	$1045.521 + e^{0.0732t}$ $R^2 = 0.3576$
Manipur	$2.4563 + e^{0.1498t}$ $R^2 = 0.9043$	$234.3691 + e^{0.1648t}$ $R^2 = 0.8945$	$59.328 + e^{0.1358t}$ $R^2 = 0.9381$
Arunachal Pradesh	$112.5371 + e^{0.1103t}$ $R^2 = 0.8426$	$26.7654 + e^{0.1365t}$ $R^2 = 0.9163$	$182.4520 + e^{0.1042t}$ $R^2 = 0.8930$
Tripura	$11.592 + e^{0.1648t}$ $R^2 = 0.9115$	$0.9437 + e^{0.1941t}$ $R^2 = 0.9031$	$44.872 + e^{0.1038t}$ $R^2 = 0.8930$

Further, higher growth of total taxes in Nagaland's situation indicates the degree of elasticity and buoyancy that are inherent in the shared taxes resulting in a larger devolution of resources from the Centre to the State by way of higher share in the Central taxes.

The data presented in column 3 of the above tables is the aggregate of the sector-wise estimates by industrial origin of the State Domestic Product at factor cost at current prices. Although the state Domestic Product in both these two states had increased in absolute terms, the exponential growth rates gives some distressing results. While the exponential growth rate of Nagaland's state domestic product stays at a lower level of 3.8 percent, the exponential growth rate of state domestic product in case of Meghalaya comes to be around 12.61 percent over the years.

If, we express the relationship between the tax revenues and state income in the conventional tax-income ratio terms, the analysis reveals some interesting results.

The percentage of State's own tax revenue to net state domestic product in the state of Meghalaya, which was 1.15 per cent in 1972-73, increased slowly over the years and stood at 4.30 per cent in 2001-02. Similarly, in Nagaland's situation, the percentage of own tax revenue to net state domestic product has almost remained comparatively static over the years. In case of Assam, the percentage of own tax revenue to net state domestic product, which was1.87 per cent in 1972-73 increased to 5.69 per cent in the year 2001-2002. If, we judge the performances of the State's own tax revenue on the basis of its contribution to the net state domestic product, then the performances of the State's own tax revenue in all the states present a poor picture altogether. The observed trend indicate the failures of both the state governments in mobilising adequate resources from its own taxation measures.

When total tax revenue is taken as a percentage of the state income, then it reveals a continuous increase in percentage share of total tax revenue in the state income over the years in both the states. This shows that over the years, a sizeable share in incremental income has been transferred to the public exchequer.

Further, an analysis of the ratio of the State's Own Tax revenue to the total tax revenues at accruing to the states during these years was carried out. A distressing feature in Naglannd's situation is that the ratio, which was 0.66 in the year 1963-64, has decreased to 0.12 in the year 2000-01. This decreasing ratio of State's Own Tax revenue to state's total tax revenue would seem to indicate that the state has not put in greater efforts than before in raising its own tax revenue in much more official way during the period from 1985-86 to 2000-01 and has not tapped more resources from the state economy thereby not increasing the avenues for financing its own expenditure. Meghalay's experience to this effect is no way different to the observed trend in the state of Nagaland. The ratio which was 0.36 in the year 1972-73 remained more or less stagnant over the years with the ratio of 0.43 in the year 2001-02. The stagnant ratio of the State's own tax revenue to the State's total tax revenue during the period of our study indicates that the State has not put in extra efforts with the passage of time in raising its own tax revenue in a much more efficient way during the thirty year period of our study and also has not made any sincere effort to tap more resources.

Thus, the inferences that follow from the above analysis are as follows:

1) There has been an increase in NSDP in all the states but the rate of increase is less than the rate of increase in State's own tax revenue and much less than the rate of increase of the total tax revenue over the period. This clearly exhibits the existence of a leakage between NSDP and resource mobilisation in these states
2) The role of the State's own tax revenue as a component of NSDP over the period of our study has not been proportionate to the likely coerce for additional taxation as a source of revenue for the State. This is substantiated by the fact that the percentage share of the State's own tax revenue in the NSDP has increased at a much slower rate than the velocity ascribed to the shared tax revenue. This raised doubt about the efficiency of state's own tax revenues

3) If, we consider tax-income ratio as the simplest measure of tax burden or sacrifice, the results of the analysis given in the forgone tables reveal that all the states under consideration fare rather poorly in their efforts to mobilise adequate sources, and

4) Lastly, it indicates the greater reliance of the states on shared taxes for the purpose of resource mobilization forced. This particular trend has all the states in the region to develop a dependency syndrome with the passage of time.

It is observed from the foregoing analysis that the rate of growth of State's Own Tax revenue is much lower than the rate of growth of the state's share in central taxes. Never the less the increasing importance of own tax revenue as an element of state income has been clearly apparent over the period in question.

Further, it is interesting to note that the relative importance of states' own tax revenue have established a somewhat erratic behavior though it has registered a trend towards an increase in all the states under consideration. It may be added here that all the states of North-Eastern region depend much more heavily on the shared taxes as the most plausible source of resource mobilisation as evident from the exponential growth rate figures of the respective states. This clearly shows the increasing dependence of the states on the central devolutions that they adhere to when compared to its otherwise increasing pressure on its own tax revenue. Thus, judged from the angle of the states' own effort, the states' revenue performance have been rather dismal in the sense that all the states raised a lower proportion of revenue in relation to the other sources of revenue, viz., shared taxes and non tax revenue.

All the above trends are corroborated by the observations that we may feel tempted to make on the basis of our analysis of Table 3.3(a) and (b).

It is observed from the foregoing Table 3.3 (a) and (b) that the rate of growth of State's Own Tax revenue is much lower than the rate of growth of the state's share in central taxes. Yet, the increasing importance of tax revenue as an element of state income has been clearly apparent over the period in question.

Tables 3.3(a) and (b) bring out the significance of trend of shared taxes for the state of Nagaland and Meghalaya for the stipulated period

Table 3.3(a): Percentage Share of State's Own Tax Revenue, Shared Taxes and Non-Tax Revenue of Nagaland, 1963-2000 (in crores)

0	1	2	3	4	5	6	7
Year	State's Own Tax Revenue	Non-Tax Revenue	Shared Taxes	Total Revenue	As % of Col.1 to Col.4	As % of Col.2 to Col.4	As % of Col.3 to Col.4
1963-64	0.06	0.13	0.03	0.22	27.27	59.09	13.64
1964-65	0.24	0.35	0.08	0.67	35.82	52.23	11.95
1965-66	0.32	0.42	0.12	0.86	37.20	48.83	13.97
1966-67	0.26	0.61	0.16	1.03	25.24	59.22	15.54
1967-68	0.35	0.59	0.17	1.11	31.53	53.15	15.32
1968-69	0.33	0.64	0.22	1.14	28.94	56.14	14.92
1969-70	0.46	1.06	0.25	1.77	25.98	59.88	14.14
1970-71	0.61	1.16	0.32	2.09	21.18	55.50	15.32
1971-72	0.75	1.19	0.34	2.28	32.89	52.19	14.92
1972-73	1.36	1.71	0.37	3.44	39.53	49.70	10.77
1973-74	1.94	1.82	0.47	4.23	45.86	43.02	11.12
1974-75	1.93	2.02	0.76	4.71	40.97	42.88	16.15
1975-76	2.86	2.31	0.89	6.06	47.20	38.11	14.69
1976-77	2.59	3.02	1.05	6.66	38.88	45.34	15.77
1977-78	2.87	3.35	1.13	7.35	39.04	45.57	15.39
1978-79	3.35	3.54	1.27	8.16	41.05	43.38	15.57

(Contd...)

0	1	2	3	4	5	6	7
1979-80	4.19	4.34	2.39	10.92	38.36	39.74	21.09
1980-81	5.19	4.92	2.64	12.75	40.70	38.58	20.72
1981-82	6.36	6.31	3.09	15.76	40.35	40.03	19.62
1982-83	7.45	9.26	3.34	20.05	37.15	46.18	16.67
1983-84	10.46	11.07	3.88	25.41	41.16	43.56	15.28
1984-85	12.46	14.81	4.26	31.53	39.51	46.97	13.52
1985-86	15.39	18.78	65.12	99.29	15.50	18.91	65.59
1986-87	15.69	24.13	70.77	110.59	14.18	21.19	64.63
1987-88	20.25	25.34	85.49	131.08	15.44	19.33	65.23
1988-89	19.49	27.17	111.30	157.96	12.33	17.20	60.48
1989-90	17.44	35.03	76.34	128.81	13.53	27.19	59.28
1990-91	18.64	31.35	119.82	169.81	10.97	18.46	70.57
1991-92	21.61	32.07	139.89	193.57	11.16	16.56	72.28
1992-93	19.75	27.37	167.12	214.24	9.21	12.77	78.02
1993-94	25.08	24.77	166.97	216.82	11.56	11.42	77.02
1994-95	25.72	85.19	187.51	298.42	8.61	28.54	62.85
1995-96	43.28	35.05	166.05	244.38	17.71	14.34	67.95
1996-97	57.06	32.55	250.24	339.85	16.78	9.57	73.65
1997-98	71.07	45.03	380.96	497.06	14.29	9.05	76.66
1998-99	61.96	44.09	410.95	519.00	11.98	8.52	79.05
1999-00	71.04	49.00	477.02	597.06	11.89	8.20	79.91
2000-01	79.00	50.08	541.94	671.02	11.77	7.46	80.77

Sources: Government of Nagaland, Finance Account (1963-64 to 1997-98);

Growth rate: Column 2 = $53.3834 + e^{.1243}t$ $R^2 = 0.56$

Growth rate: Column 3 = $26.850 + e^{.1705}t$ $R^2 = 0.45$

Growth rate: Column 4 = $70.7161 + e^{.1695}t$ $R^2 = 0.51$

covered by the study. It is observed that the share of shared taxes in the total revenue of the states have increased steadily over the years in both the states. However, a look at the column 5 and 7 of the above tables reveal

Table 3.3(b): Percentage Shares of State's Own Tax Revenue Shared Taxes and Non-tax Revenue of Meghalaya

(Rupees in Crores)

Year	State's Own Tax	Non-Tax Revenue	Shared Taxes	Total Revenue	Col.2 to As % of Col.5	Col.3 to As % of Col.5	Col.4 to As % of Col.5
0	1	2	3	4	5	6	7
1972-73	1.21	0.93	2.12	4.26	28.40	21.83	49.77
1973-74	1.55	1.27	2.31	5.13	30.21	24.76	45.03
1974-75	1.95	1.98	2.23	6.16	31.66	32.14	36.20
1975-76	2.18	3.04	2.92	8.14	26.78	37.35	35.87
1976-77	2.48	2.14	3.09	7.71	32.17	27.76	40.07
1977-78	2.58	2.04	3.24	7.86	32.83	25.95	41.22
1978-79	3.39	4.14	3.58	11.11	30.51	37.27	32.22
1979-80	4.04	3.65	6.52	14.21	28.43	25.69	45.88
1980-81	4.88	21.93	7.18	33.99	14.36	64.52	21.12
1981-82	6.20	6.34	8.02	20.56	30.15	30.84	39.01
1982-83	7.37	5.99	8.72	22.08	33.38	27.13	39.49
1983-84	9.50	7.21	9.86	26.57	35.75	27.14	37.11
1984-85	12.24	9.79	10.67	32.70	37.43	29.94	32.63
1985-86	14.93	11.51	45.52	71.96	20.75	15.99	63.26
1986-87	17.74	14.11	55.27	87.12	20.36	16.20	63.44
1987-88	19.61	17.26	65.29	102.16	19.19	16.90	63.91
1988-89	27.72	20.90	82.47	131.09	21.15	15.94	62.91
1989-90	32.26	18.85	65.17	116.28	27.74	16.21	56.05
1990-91	36.01	18.71	80.36	135.08	26.66	13.85	59.49
1991-92	42.54	22.62	105.27	170.43	24.96	13.27	61.77
1992-93	44.18	18.08	125.64	187.90	23.51	9.62	66.87
1993-94	47.93	28.40	127.83	204.16	23.48	13.91	62.61
1994-95	56.27	38.64	144.63	239.54	23.49	16.13	60.38
1995-96	66.26	66.92	159.71	292.89	22.62	22.85	54.53
1996-97	77.37	47.47	217.56	342.40	22.60	13.86	63.54
1997-98	73.55	29.85	286.77	390.17	18.85	7.65	73.50
1998-99	88.36	51.46	300.55	440.37	20.06	11.69	68.25
1999-00	102.98	83.86	341.76	528.60	19.48	15.87	64.65
2000-01	132.48	95.48	164.25	392.21	33.78	24.34	41.88
2001-02	140.45	105.35	183.16	428.96	32.74	24.56	42.70

Source:Budget in Brief, Government of Meghalaya:: 1974-75; 1977-78; 1978-79; 1982-83; 1983-84 *Budget at a Glance,* Government of Meghalaya:: 1984-85; 1989-90; 1994-95; 1996-97; 1998-99; 2001-02

Rate of Growth : Column 2 = $1.3438\ e^{0.1444t}$ $R^2 = 0.9191$
Column 3 = $1.4510\ e^{0.1955t}$ $R^2 = 0.9385$
Column 4 = $4.0045\ e^{0.1761t}$ $R^2 = 0.9673$

that the relative importance of states' own taxes have been much less than it has been in the case of shared taxes as an element of total revenue of the states over the period in question.

Further, it is interesting to note that the relative importance of states' own tax revenue have established a somewhat erratic behavior though it has registered a trend towards an increase in both the states under consideration.

It may be added here that both the states of Nagaland and Meghalaya depend much more heavily on the shared taxes as the most plausible source of resource mobilisation as evident from the exponential growth rate figures of the respective states. This clearly shows the increasing dependence of the states on the central devolutions that they dependent upon when compared to its otherwise increasing pressure on its own tax revenue. Thus, judged from the angle of the states' own effort, the states' revenue performance have been rather dismal in the sense that both the states raised a lower proportion of revenue in relation to the other sources of revenue, viz., shared taxes and non tax revenue.

3. 5 Average and Marginal Tax Rate

The methods followed to estimate both Average and Marginal tax rates have already been discussed in details in chapter 2 of this book.

Tables 3.4(a) and (b) are an attempt to present the average and marginal tax rate not only for aggregate revenue but also for shared taxes and state's own tax revenues. We consider these two tables as an improvement of Table 3.1(a) and (b) as they provide some further insight into the changing tax-income ratio over a period of time.

The analysis of average and marginal tax rates that we carried out are not only for the aggregate revenue but also for shared taxes and State's Own Tax revenue.

The finding based on the above analysis reveals that the

average tax rate in case of State's Own Tax revenue in all the states has recorded a uniform pattern in the entire plan periods covered by our study. It suggests that for all practical purposes, there exited a shift in the pattern of tax revenue since the fiscal year 1985-86. And, by and large, the average tax rate seems to have registered a moderate increase for the State's Own Tax revenue and a spectacular increase for the shared taxes.

Further, the segmentation of the total tax revenue into those accruing to the State's Own Taxes and shared taxes, respectively, clearly suggest that the bulk of the increase in the overall revenues has to be accounted for shared taxes. On an average, out of the 22 per cent of the state's income taken away by the State and the Union Government in the year 1998-99, 1.90 per cent was by the Union Government alone and the rest 2.60 per cent by the State Government. In other words, the Union has collected more than 88 per cent of the total revenue, and the contribution of the State, itself, was only 12 per cent.

A closer perusal of the said Tables suggests that there existed a shift in the pattern of tax revenue of both the states. For instance, the Average Tax Rate in the both the states seems to have registered a moderate increase for the state's own tax revenue and a spectacular increase for the shared taxes.

Further, the division of the total tax revenues into those accruing to the State's own taxes and shared taxes, clearly shows that in case of both the states, the bulk of the increase in the total tax revenue is accounted for by the shared taxes.

A closer look at column 2 of the table 3.4b indicates that of the 18.03 per cent of the net state domestic product taken away by the State of Meghalaya and the Centre in the year 1999-2000 towards resource mobilisations, 13.86 per cent is by the Centre alone, and the rest 4.17 per cent by the State government. In other words, the Union Government has

Table 3.4(a): Average and Marginal Rates of taxation in Nagaland from 1963-64 to 1998-99 (in crores)

0	1	2	3	4	5	6
	Average Tax Rate on			Marginal Tax Rate on		
Year	Total Tax Rev.	State's Own Tax Rev.	Shared Taxes	Total Tax Rev.	State's Own Tax Rev.	Shared Taxes
1963-64	1.50	1.00	0.50	-	-	-
1964-65	3.60	2.70	0.90	7.93	6.20	1.73
1965-66	3.10	2.30	0.80	2.30	1.50	0.80
1966-67	2.60	1.60	1.00	-0.86	-2.60	1.73
1967-68	2.80	1.90	0.90	4.30	3.90	0.40
1968-69	2.60	1.50	1.10	1.20	-0.08	2.00
1969-70	3.20	2.00	1.20	13.32	10.83	2.50
1970-71	3.70	2.40	1.30	8.14	5.55	2.59
1971-72	3.80	2.60	1.20	4.50	4.00	0.50
1972-73	4.80	3.80	1.00	8.76	8.30	0.46
1973-74	5.80	4.60	1.10	11.52	9.80	1.72
1974-75	5.40	3.90	1.50	3.60	-0.12	3.72
1975-76	6.60	5.00	1.50	14.11	12.40	1.71
1976-77	5.60	4.00	1.60	-1.52	-3.70	2.18
1977-78	5.40	3.90	1.50	0.80	3.00	0.80
1978-79	5.30	3.80	1.40	4.60	3.50	1.10

(Contd...)

0	1	2	3	4	5	6
1979-80	6.00	3.80	2.10	8.60	3.70	4.85
1980-81	5.90	3.90	1.90	5.40	4.30	1.10
1981-82	5.70	3.80	1.80	5.22	3.70	1.52
1982-83	5.20	3.50	1.60	3.60	2.40	1.20
1983-84	5.60	4.10	1.50	7.45	6.30	1.15
1984-85	7.20	5.30	1.80	-	-	-
1985-86	31.00	5.80	25.20	214.78	9.80	204.98
1986-87	29.00	4.60	24.40	18.14	0.09	18.05
1987-88	31.20	6.00	25.30	45.04	10.36	34.68
1988-89	36.20	5.30	30.80	107.56	-3.20	110.71
1989-90	21.16	4.00	17.60	-51.60	-2.80	-48.80
1990-91	20.80	2.80	18.00	19.40	0.52	18.88
1991-92	21.12	2.80	18.30	23.20	3.00	20.20
1992-93	22.20	2.30	19.80	31.71	2.32	29.39
1993-94	21.80	2.80	18.90	13.60	14.02	-0.42
1994-95	16.90	2.00	14.80	5.58	0.16	5.42
1995-96	12.60	2.60	10.00	-0.98	4.42	-5.40
1996-97	16.60	3.00	13.50	50.86	7.15	43.71
1997-98	21.10	3.30	17.80	50.20	4.85	45.35
1998-99	21.60	2.80	18.80	44.40	-19.37	63.77

Sources: Table 3.1(a) and 3.2 (a)

Table 3.4 (b) AVERAGE and Marginal Rates of Taxation in meghalaya for the PERIOD 1972-73 to 2001-2002

Year	Total Tax Rev.	State's Own Tax Rev.	Shared Taxes	Total Tax Rev.	State's Own Tax Rev.	Shared Taxes
0	1	2	3	4	5	6
1972-73	3.17	1.15	2.02	16.21	10.40	5.81
1973-74	3.56	1.43	2.13	8.86	11.08	- 2.22
1974-75	3.73	1.74	1.99	25.99	6.50	19.49
1975-76	4.42	1.89	2.53	10.28	6.56	3.72
1976-77	4.64	2.07	2.57	1.70	0.68	1.02
1977-78	4.32	1.91	2.41	7.66	5.39	2.27
1978-79	4.65	2.26	2.39	22.88	4.14	18.74
1979-80	6.38	2.44	3.94	10.66	5.93	4.73
1980-81	6.72	2.72	4.00	8.24	5.03	3.21
1981-82	6.91	3.01	3.90	8.75	5.50	3.25
1982-83	7.08	3.25	3.83	9.07	5.91	3.16
1983-84	7.36	3.61	3.75	9.07	7.00	2.07
1984-85	7.58	4.05	3.53	95.62	6.85	88.77
1985-86	17.70	4.37	13.33	28.06	6.28	21.78
1986-87	18.90	4.59	14.31	14.77	2.32	12.45
1987-88	18.19	4.20	13.99	64.65	20.74	43.91
1988-89	21.78	5.48	16.30	- 8.24	2.26	10.50
1989-90	14.78	4.73	10.05	17.52	4.47	13.05
1990-91	15.17	4.69	10.48	26.90	5.59	21.31
1991-92	16.72	4.81	11.91	23.34	1.74	21.60
1992-93	17.35	4.51	12.84	14.21	2.42	11.79
1993-94	15.51	4.23	11.28	4.76	6.69	- 1.93
1994-95	15.97	4.47	11.50	20.50	8.17	12.33
1995-96	16.37	4.80	11.57	65.70	10.58	55.12
1996-97	19.86	5.21	14.65	31.87	- 1.86	33.74
1997-98	21.32	4.35	16.97	7.35	3.81	3.54
1998-99	18.70	4.25	14.45	14.39	3.77	10.62
1999-00	18.03	4.17	13.86	- 43.65	8.70	- 52.35
2000-01	10.57	4.72	5.85	5.83	1.73	4.10
2001-02	9.90	4.30	5.60			

Note : Calculations are based on Tables 3.1(b) and 3.2(b)

collected more than 77 per cent of the total revenue, and the contribution of the State itself is only 23 per cent. It can be seen that throughout the thirty year period of our study, only the year 1984-85 witnessed the contribution of the State's own taxes to be slightly higher than the contribution of shared taxes. This means that, the contribution of the State's own taxes declined from 36.28 per cent in the year 1972-73 to 23.13 per cent in 1999-2000. We may note it here that although, the year 200-2001 and 2001-2002, experienced some improvements in these tax rates, we can not draw any definite conclusion out of it, due to the fact that, figures represented against this particular year was the budget estimate. And, to that extent, our conclusion, if drawn, might be adversely affected.

On the other hand, for the state of Nagaland, the division of the total tax revenue into those accruing to the State's Own Taxes and shared taxes, respectively, clearly suggests that the bulk of the increase in the overall revenues has to be accounted for shared taxes. Of the 21.60 per cent of the state's income (column 2 of the table) taken away by the State and the Union Government in the year 1998-99, 18.80 per cent was by the Union Government alone and the rest 2.80 per cent by the State Government. In other words, the Union has collected more than 87 per cent of the total revenue, and the contribution of the State, itself, was only 13 per cent.

Thus, the results obtained from the above exercises suggest that during the specific period covered by the study for the states of Nagaland and Meghalaya, consistent and deliberate efforts on the part of the central government in comparison to the state governments, which has accounted for a substantial part of variations in the marginal tax rate under these heads.

The findings based on the above observations suggest that the increased tax burden in both the states during the period of study has come primarily through the central goverment. Thus, if we look at the problem from the point of view of Average and Marginal Tax Rate, it may be concluded that both the states have made relatively lower tax efforts to mobilise adequate internal resources to meet its growing developmental needs.

Thus, it is evident that both the states have performed rather poorly in mobilizing adequate resources from their internal sources for the purpose of carrying out their own developmental plan programmes. This trend no doubt talks about the poor resource base of these two economies. Therefore, in the absence of additional means to mop up adequate revenue, both the states are far from goal of financial self-reliance, which has necessitated them, to depend much more heavily on the federal transfer to meet the growing demand for public expenditure. As a result of the intensified adherence to the principle of fiscal deficiency, the states of Meghalaya and Nagaland have shown a distinct trend of rapidly growing financial dependence on federal transfers. Bearing in mind this ground reality, an attempt is made to ascertain the compositional magnitude of the total Central transfers in the over all State finances. Given the poor resource base of these two representative states, we think it imperative to study the quantitative implications of federal transfers to these two states in order to find out how far the relative yield of various components of public resources has remained consistent with the requirements of rapid economic development. Accordingly, an attempt is made in the following paragraphs to examine the magnitude and the components of federal transfers to the states in n order to find out their relative size and importance in the overall fiscal structure of the state.

3.1.6 Trends and Patternns of Fiscal Tranfer

The intention here is to examine the trends in the composition of federal transfers with reference to its main components, namely,. (i) tax devolution, that is state's share of the central taxes as determined by the recommendations of the Finance Commission, (ii) grants –in aid of different Categories and (iii) Central Loans. This exercise is carried out with a motive to determine and ascertain the total quantum of resources that are made available to the respective state governments in order to carry out their various developmental plan programmes.

The tables 3.5(a) and (b) indicate that the total Central resources transferred to the State of Meghalaya in absolute terms were Rs. 20.71 crores in 1972-73, which increased to Rs. 1136.21 crores in 2001-02. Similarly, the total resources transferred to the state of Nagaland, which was Rs.7.50 crores during the Third plan period increased to Rs.1118 crores during the IX plan period. The ratio of Union resources transferred to aggregate State's expenditure no doubt suggests a state of apathy towards the resource mobilisation capacity of the individual states. Looking at the problem from this angle itself speaks out the internal resource constraints that the North-Eastern States experience in recent years. The ratio of Union resources transferred to aggregate states' expenditure in Meghalaya which was at 62.29 per cent in 1972-73 increased to 63.65 per cent in 2001-02. This ratio which was at 82 percent in Nagaland during the 3rd.plan period slightly decreased to 78 percent during the 9th. Plan period. The experiences of all other states are no way different from the experiences of the states of Nagaland and Meghalaya.

Table: 3.5 (a) Total Transfer of Financial Resources from the Union to the State of Nagaland (1963-64 to 2000-01)

(Rs. In crores)

	III Plan 1963-64 to 1965-66	IV Plan 1069-70 to 1973-74	V Plan 1974-75 to 1978-79	VI Plan 1980-81 to 1984-85	VII Plan 1985-86 to 1989-90	VIII Plan 1992-93 to 1996-97	IX Plan 1997-98 to 200-01
1. share of Divisible taxes and Duties	0.07(1)	0.35(1)	1.02(1.85)	3.44(2)	81.80(23)	187.57(30)	452.71(40)
2. Grants-in-aid	7.42(98)	26.21(82)	46.69(84)	120.99(62)	213.02(62)	397.59(59)	538.10(48)
a) Statutory (within the purview of Finance Commission)	1.96(26)	16.66(64)	29.67 (63.54)	59.20(49)	46.38(21)	143.43(36)	-
b) Other grants (Within the purview of Planning Commission and F.C.)	5.46(72)	12.11(36)	17.02(36.46)	61.79(51)	166.63(79)	254.15(64)	-
3. loan	1.00(1)	5.30(17)	7.31(14.15)	17.98(13)	48.51(15)	85.12(11)	127.19(12)

4	Total Federal Transfer	7.50(100)	31.86(100)	55.02(100)	142.41 (100)	343.33 (100)	670.98 (100)	1118.00 (100)
5.	Total statutory transfer	2.03(27)	17.01(53)	30.69(95)	62.64(44)	128.18 (37)	331.00(49)	-
6.	Total non-Statutory Transfer	5.47(73)	14.85(47)	24.33(45)	79.77(56)	215.14 (630	339.97(51)	-
7.	State's own Resources (Tax and Non Tax).	0.50	2.40	5.56	17.68	43.74	70.01	117.81
8.	Aggregate state's Expenditure	9.13	35.43	83.96	186.31	421.20	948.63	1428.62
9.	Total Resources transfer to aggregate state Expenditure	82%	90%	65%	76%	81.!5%	70%	78%

Note: Figures in parentheses indicate the proportion to total

Sources: Finance Accounts of Nagaland (1963-64 to 1969-70 and 1976-77 to 1998-1999) , CMIE,2000 and Statistical Abstract of Nagaland, 1968, 1970,1975,2000.

TABLE: 3.5(b) Transfer of Financial Resources from the Union to the State of Meghalaya

(Rupees in Crores)

Year	Shared Taxes	Total statutory grants	Loans & Advances from the Centre	Total Resources transferred	State's Total Own Resources (Tax & Non-Tax)	Aggregate State's Expenditure	Total Resource Transferred to Aggregate State's Expenditure	State's Total Own Resources to Aggregate State's Expenditure
0	1	2	3	4	5	6	7	8
1972-73	2.12 (10.24)	13.23 (63.88)	5.36 (25.88)	20.71 (100.00)	2.14	33.25	62.29	6.44
1973-74	2.31 (11.58)	12.18 (61.05)	5.46 (27.37)	19.95 (100.00)	2.82	26.86	74.27	10.50
1974-75	2.23 (8.49)	23.39 (89.07)	0.64 (2.44)	26.26 (100.00)	3.92	32.69	80.33	11.99
1975-76	2.92 (10.03)	25.19 (86.53)	1.00 (3.44)	29.11 (100.00)	5.22	35.44	82.14	14.73
1976-77	3.09 (8.62)	30.82 (85.97)	1.94 (5.41)	35.85 (100.00)	4.62	40.95	87.55	11.28
1977-78	3.24 (8.26)	33.46 (85.36)	2.50 (6.38)	39.20 (100.00)	4.62	56.18	69.78	8.22
1978-79	3.59 (7.21)	43.90 (88.12)	2.33 (4.67)	49.82 (100.00)	7.53	55.29	90.11	13.62

1979-80	6.52 (11.94)	46.19 (84.58)	1.90 (3.48)	54.61 (100.00)	7.69	64.19	85.08	11.98
1980-81	7.19 (10.70)	55.94 (83.27)	4.05 (6.03)	67.18 (100.00)	26.81	101.94	65.90	26.30
1981-82	8.03 (10.72)	61.81 (82.52)	5.06 (6.76)	74.90 (100.00)	12.54	136.57	54.84	9.18
1982-83	8.73 (8.08)	74.71 (69.10)	24.67 (22.82)	108.11 (100.00)	13.36	124.71	86.69	10.71
1983-84	9.86 (8.35)	98.39 (83.28)	9.89 (8.37)	118.14 (100.00)	16.71	147.01	80.36	11.37
1984-85	10.67 (7.80)	115.28 (84.28)	10.83 (7.92)	136.78 (100.00)	22.03	178.29	76.72	12.36
1985-86	45.52 (26.85)	111.02 (65.48)	13.00 (7.67)	169.54 (100.00)	26.44	191.93	88.33	13.78
1986-87	55.27 (28.20)	127.54 (65.07)	13.18 (6.73)	195.99 (100.00)	31.85	230.22	85.13	13.83
1987-88	65.29 (27.74)	154.29 (65.55)	15.78 (6.71)	235.36 (100.00)	36.88	264.36	89.03	13.95
1988-89	82.47 (29.83)	171.18 (61.92)	22.79 (8.25)	276.44 (100.00)	48.62	318.05	86.92	15.29
1989-90	65.17 (22.17)	192.82 (65.58)	36.02 (12.25)	294.01 (100.00)	50.05	350.69	83.84	14.27
1990-91	80.36 (24.64)	217.89 (66.81)	27.87 (8.55)	326.12 (100.00)	54.72	405.65	80.39	13.49

(Contd...)

0	1	2	3	4	5	6	7	8
1991-92	105.27	238.25	20.74	364.26	65.17	492.29	73.99	13.24
	(28.90)	(65.41)	(5.69)	(100.00)				
1992-93	125.64	240.60	22.19	388.43	62.26	588.60	65.99	10.58
	(32.35)	(61.94)	(5.71)	(100.00)				
1993-94	127.82	296.63	105.41	529.86	76.33	909.08	58.29	8.40
	(24.12)	(55.98)	(19.90)	(100.00)				
1994-95	144.63	290.76	37.50	472.89	94.92	796.20	59.39	11.92
	(30.58)	(61.49)	(7.93)	(100.00)				
1995-96	159.71	391.00	20.87	571.58	133.18	796.41	71.77	16.72
	(27.94)	(68.41)	(3.65)	(100.00)				
1996-97	217.57	388.06	28.53	634.16	124.84	813.58	77.95	15.34
	(34.31)	(61.19)	(4.50)	(100.00)				
1997-98	286.77	306.58	39.42	632.77	103.40	850.72	74.38	12.15
	(45.32)	(48.45)	(6.23)	(100.00)				
1998-99	300.55	392.32	48.88	741.75	139.82	1022.93	72.51	13.67
	(40.52)	(52.89)	(6.59)	(100.00)				
1999-00	341.76	415.04	50.76	807.56	186.85	1195.40	67.56	15.63
	(42.32)	(51.39)	(6.29)	(100.00)				
2000-01*	164.25	845.01	61.31	1070.57	227.96	1601.89	66.83	14.23
	(15.34)	(78.93)	(5.73)	(100.00)				
2001-02**	183.16	892.17	60.88	1136.21	245.80	1785.15	63.65	13.77
	(16.12)	(78.52)	(5.36)	(100.00)				

Note :
* = Revised Estimate
** = Budget Estimate
Shared taxes include (i) share of income tax proceeds, and (ii) share of proceeds from Union excise duties.
Source : Budget in Brief, Government of Meghalaya:: 1974-75; 1977-78; 1978-79; 1982-83; 1983-84; Budget at a Glance, Government of Meghalaya:: 1984-85; 1986-87; 1989-90; 1996-97; 2000-01; 2001-2002

If the pattern of the composition of federal transfers is to be taken as the yardstick to measure the relative degree of self-reliance of the States, then the findings of the foregoing analysis corroborate the inferences drawn earlier that the degree of self-reliance in North-Eastern states is exceptionally low. This is further supported by all the North-Eastern states' remarkably high dependence on grants, the high and increasing share of tax devolution, and the relatively small share of their own taxes and non-tax revenue in the overall resource mobilisation effort of the States.

3.7 Concluding Remarks

The analysis of the ratio of the State's own tax revenue to the total tax revenues accruing to the State was an attempt to ascertain the degree of tax efforts of the government during these years. It is quite disheartening to note that the ratio has nearly remained stagnant during the period of our study. In the light of the above finding, we may conclude that the States had neither put in extra efforts in raising its own tax revenue in a much more efficient way nor had it made any sincere effort to tap more resources during the period covered by our study. We believe, this might have been one of the factors responsible for the explosive cycles of public expenditure growth.

The important findings of this chapter are as follows.

An analysis of the percentage share of state's total tax revenue and shared taxes in the net state domestic product exhibited some disturbing results. The percentage of State's own tax revenue to net state domestic product, increased slowly over the years in case of both the states. If, we judge the performances of the State's own tax revenue on the basis of its contribution to State income, then the performances of the State's own tax revenue presents a poor picture altogether. From this point of view, the State's own tax revenue has been increasing at a very slow rate during the period of our study. If we visualize tax-income ratio as the simplest measure of tax burden or sacrifice then the analysis revealed that the ratio has marginally increased in all the three states of Assam, Nagaland and Meghalaya implying thereby the non-existence of a dynamic tax structure over the years. This only proves that the States of North-Eastern region fare rather poorly on this count.

Based on the above exercises, we may be tempted to conclude that, the trend observed from the pattern of the composition of the State's taxes is not at all warranted from the point of view of a healthy fiscal economy. The reverse would have been commendable in the context of the State's efforts at achieving self-reliance with regard to resource mobilization of adequate resources for implementing several developmental programmes.

Thus, we may say that there are two policy implications, which emerges from these exercises.

From the above findings, we may be tempted to draw two inferences. First, in the absence of any cohesive additional domestic resource mobilization programmes, financing of ever increasing public expenditure has led to the dependency syndrome of the State on the Centre for higher grants-in-aid. Secondly, the non-existence of a vibrant tax structure in order to finance the increased volume of public expenditure has placed these States at the mercy of market forces in terms of public borrowings. Judged from the angle of sound fiscal ethics, the performance of the State governments to this effect seems to be unreasonable, and unwarranted.

In order to find out the extent of dependency of the State on the contribution of Central taxes, an analysis of the shared taxes in the total tax revenue of the State revealed that the shared taxes have increased in all the states on an average from 30.02 per cent in the year 1972-73 to 71.85 per cent in the year 1998-1999. A striking feature of the State's taxation as revealed by our analysis was the phenomenal increase in contribution of the shared taxes to the total tax revenue of the State. It was observed that over the years, there has been a continual outpacing of the State's own tax revenue by the shared taxes. This indicated that the relative importance of the State's own taxes has been much less than it has been in the case of shared taxes as a component of total tax revenue of the State during the period of our study. As a result, the States have cut a poor figure with regard to the efforts put in by it during the last thirty years of our study to mop up additional resources from its own sources. The increasing dependence of the State on the share of Central taxes might partly be due to the ever-increasing pressure of the State on the Central Government to widen the pool of shareable taxes and partly due to the greater in-built flexibility and in-built responsiveness that have been brought into these taxes thereby making them more elastic and buoyant than the State's own taxes.

If the resource constraints imposed on the states can alternatively be viewed as the failures of the state governments to finance its ever-increasing public expenditure growth, then the question arises, what have been the cosequnces of public expenditure growth in these states? This, we intend to accomplish in the next Chapter.

CHAPTER– IV

PUBLIC EXPENDITURE POLICIES

4.1 Introduction

This chapter is concerned with an analytical and critical evaluation of the expenditure policies of North-Eastern States, during the period 1963-64 to 2000-2001. Such an analysis is sought in terms of the trends and patterns of the States' Public expenditure. The purpose of this chapter is to study, what were the overall trends in states' public expenditures and the direction in which it has moved in the last thirty eight years of planning. Ultimately, it is the size and composition of public expenditures that the community looks to.

Further, an attempt is made to discuss the utilisation pattern of public resources in the two representative states of Nagaland and Meghalaya. Such an analysis is sought in terms of the patterns of public expenditure /public investment outlays and their growth over the years.

4.2. Thrust of the Problem

The observed phenomenon in the North-Eastern region's context exhibits a tremendous increase in public investment outlays over the years. In order to understand the intricacies of the problem of resource urtlisation in the context of the two representative states of North-East, it is proper to analyse first the trends of public expenditure or the direction in which it has moved. Keeping this in mind, an attempt is made here to discuss the growth of total public expenditure both revenue and capital accounts of the two states for the period under investigation.

4.3 Growth of Aggregate Public Expenditure

The following Tables 4.1(a) and 4.1(b) present the trend of the growth of total public expenditure for the states of Nagaland and Meghalaya respectively.

A close perusal at Column 1 of the Tables given below exhibits that total public expenditure in case of both the states has increased several folds over the years. The average annual rate of increase in the total public expenditure worked out to be 120.45 percent and 117.65 percent for the state of Nagaland and Meghalaya respectively for the period 1972-73 to 2000-2001.

Column 2 of the above tables shows the growth of net state domestic product which has increased from Rs. 105.09 crores in 1972-73 to Rs. 3267.36 crores in 2001-02 maintaining an average annual rate of increase of 100.30 per cent in the state of Meghalaya. On the other hand, there has been a tremendous increase in Nagaland's State domestic product from 35.6 crores to 2183.8 crores thereby registering an average annual rate of increase of 208.07 percent during the time period 1972-73 to 2000-01.

Thus, it may be inferred that the average annual rate of increase of total public expenditure in both the states outweigh the average annual rate of increase in net state domestic product. Thus, we find that Government expenditure has grown at a faster rate than the State income.

Column 3 of the Tables indicates total public expenditure as a percentage of net state domestic product. It is interesting to note that while the percentage share of total public expenditure to state domestic prduct gives an erratic trend in case of Nagaland, a smooth trend is observed to this effect in case of the state of Meghalaya. In absolute terms, although the ratio of total public expenditure to state domestic product has increased several folds from 48.9 percent to 68.2 and 31.64 to 54.64 in case of the states of Nagaland and Meghalaya respectively, in relative terms, both the percentages have increased more or less in same proportions and in same magnitudes.

Table 4.1 (a) Total Receipts and Expenditures and State Income of Nagaland (in crores)

Year	*Total Expenditures*	*NSDP*	*% of (1) to (2)*
(0)	(1)	(2)	(3)
1963-64	2.89	5.9	48.9
1964-65	10.55	8.7	121.2
1965-66	13.96	13.8	101.1
1966-67	16.37	16.1	10.16
1967-68	21.38	18.4	116.1
1968-69	23.81	20.9	113.9
1969-70	26.38	22.1	119.3
1970-71	31.83	24.8	128.3
1971-72	38.20	28.3	134.9
1972-73	40.36	35.6	113.3
1973-74	40.40	41.5	97.3
1974-75	48.60	49.2	9.87
1975-76	67.99	56.7	119.9
1976-77	84.58	63.9	132.3
1977-78	98.01	73.2	133.8

(Contd...)

(0)	(1)	(2)	(3)
1978-79	120.64	86.6	139.3
1979-80	107.43	109.2	98.3
1980-81	137.09	132.3	103.6
1981-82	158.46	163.3	97.0
1982-83	245.15	207.5	118.1
1983-84	310.31	255.1	121.6
1984-85	243.52	231.4	105.2
1985-86	344.65	261.1	131.9
1986-87	385.33	293.9	131.1
1987-88	439.93	337.9	130.1
1988-89	469.05	361.2	129.8
1989-90	517.07	432.9	119.4
1990-91	548.42	662.5	82.7
1991-92	716.45	761.50	09.0
1992-93	776.94	841.5	92.3
1993-94	905.37	879.5	102.9
1994-95	853.83	1258.7	67.8
1995-96	1079.22	1655.9	65.1
1996-97	1127.83	1848.5	61.0
1997-98	1230.30	2136.8	57.5
1998-99	1490.50	2183.8	68.2
1999-00	1494.90	-	-
2000-01	1498.80	-	-

*Source:*Finance Accounts of Nagaland; Statistical Handbook of Nagaland, 1968, 1970,1975,1980, 1986, 1990, 1996, 1997, 2000; and Estimates of Net State Domestic Poduct 2000.

Table 4.1 (b) Growth of Total Public Expenditure of the state of Meghalaya

Year	State's Total Expen-diture(Te) (Rs. Crore)	Net State Domestic Product (Rs. Crore)	Column2 as a percentage of Col.3
(0)	(1)	(2)	(3)
1972-73	33.25	105.09	31.64
1973-74	26.86	108.36	24.79
1974-75	32.69	111.97	29.20
1975-76	35.44	115.51	30.68
1976-77	40.95	120.08	34.10
1977-78	56.18	134.75	41.69
1978-79	55.29	149.77	36.92
1979-80	64.19	165.46	38.79
1980-81	101.94	179.62	56.75
1981-82	136.57	205.84	66.35
1982-83	124.71	227.10	54.91
1983-84	147.01	263.14	55.87
1984-85	178.30	302.27	58.99
1985-86	191.93	341.53	56.20
1986-87	230.22	386.25	59.60
1987-88	264.36	466.86	56.63

(Contd...)

(0)	(1)	(2)	(3)
1988-89	318.05	505.96	62.86
1989-90	350.69	659.78	53.15
1990-91	405.65	767.35	52.86
1991-92	492.29	884.22	55.68
1992-93	588.60	978.54	60.15
1993-94	909.08	1133.38	80.21
1994-95	777.97	1258.04	61.84
1995-96	796.42	1380.31	57.70
1996-97	813.58	1485.28	54.78
1997-98	850.72	1690.42	50.33
1998-99	1022.93	2079.25	49.20
1999-00	1195.40	2467.13	48.45
2000-01	1601.89 (R.E.)	2806.20	57.08
2001-02	1785.15 (B.E.)	3267.36	54.64

Source : Budget in Brief, Government of Meghalaya, 1974-75; 1977-78; 1978-79, *Budget at a Glance,* Government of Meghalaya:: 1984-85; 1986-87; 1987-88; 1989-90; 1992-93; 1993-94; 1994-95; 1996-97;1998-99; 2001-2002,*Statistical Hand Book,* Meghalaya,1976

Estimates of State Domestic Product of Meghalaya, 1980-81 to 1995-96, Government of Meghalaya, Directorate of Economics and Statistics, Meghalaya, Shillong,

State Economy, Government of Meghalaya, Directorate of Economics and Statistics

The growth in public expenditure as seen above may be explained by the intensive development effor's made by the government through its various planning periods. It suggests that the level of developmental efforts of the states and the level of public expenditure has remained complementary to each other. Further, a well planned and well visualised pattern of public expenditure not only help in developing the sectors of the economy but also provides an incentive for the simultaneous development of their sub-sectors.

The factors responsible for expanding public sector activities in the States' economy can be explained through two distinct approaches. The first approach relates to the increasing pressure on the demand for public services so as to create a reasonable degree of fiscal illusion, which become a necessary condition for mobilisation of necessary resources for furthering the process of economic development. In a growing economy which is characterized by social welfare norms, public expenditure is bound to increase with the changing needs and aspirations of its growing population. Further, a growing economy needs the development of sound economic infrastructure that certainly puts a pressure on public resources.

The second approach is based on the supply factor. In an economy where the private sector's active participation is under nourished, the public sector has to play a decisive role in shaping and re-shaping the structure of the economy.

Thus, both demand and supply factors taken together might have made a decisive influence on expanding the public sector size in these economies.

Further, an attempt is made to calculate the exponential growth rate of the economic variables presented in the above tables by using the following the earlier method ($y=ae^{rt}$). The compound growth rates for both the total expenditure and state domestic product are presented below for comparative purposes.

Nagaland	Meghalaya
$T_e = 906.62^{e0.146896t}$, $R^2=0.97$	$Te = 23.7504^{e0.1468t}$; $R^2 = 0.9851$
$NSDP = 2025.308 + e0.038t, R2 = 0.14$	$NSDP = 66.2490^{e0.1261t}$; $R^2 = 0.9889$

It is observed from the above estimating equations that

the exponential growth rate of the total public expenditure in both the states surpasses the growth of state income during the period covered by our study.

4.4 Compositional Pattern of Public Expenditure

Since the growth of aggregate public expenditure does not tell us about the direction of compositional pattern of public expenditure, we thought it imperative to segregate the total public outlays in to Revenue and Capital outlays for the purpose of getting a clear picture about the direction of change in the compositional patterns of total public outlays.

Keeping this in view, an attempt is made in the following paragraphs to present the composition and the growth of revenue expenditure of the state under three heads namely, General services, Social services, and Economic services. The compositional pattern of the revenue expenditure for the state of Meghalaya and Nagaland are presented in Table 4. 2(a) and (b) respectively.

It is evident from Tables 4..2(a) and (b) that the revenue expenditures under the various heads in both the states have increased tremendously over the years. An anatomy of the revenue expenditures exhibits the following specific directions.

It is evident from the above tables a major portion of total revenue expenditure has entered into the non developmental expenditure under General services where it stayed at near about 46 percent of the total revenue expenditure. The reasons for the tremendous increase of non-developmental expenditure being the expansion of the state administrative machinery; the steady increase in the emoluments of government servants necessitated by rise in prices and the mounting interest payments and servicing of debts, etc. The observed trend indicates the rapid expansion of the service sector which has taken place in both the states over the years.

Table 4 .2 (a) Sector-wise Revenue Expenditure of Meghalaya

(Rupees in Crore)

Year	General Services	Social Services	Economic Services
0	1	2	3
1972-73	5.01	6.15	7.02
1973-74	4.96	6.62	7.97
1974-75	7.61	7.00	10.42
1975-76	8.98	7.91	10.47
1976-77	8.61	9.00	12.51
1977-78	12.69	13.03	15.49
1978-79	10.72	12.28	17.40
1979-80	11.52	14.29	20.14
1980-81	16.71	19.49	25.62
1981-82	21.94	24.81	27.53
1982-83	28.10	29.07	27.85
1983-84	27.61	37.89	34.22
1984-85	30.78	31.78	44.76
1985-86	33.07	44.30	52.60
1986-87	47.98	48.86	59.58
1987-88	57.60	56.82	75.19
1988-89	68.38	76.61	79.59
1989-90	78.58	94.86	85.33
1990-91	87.58	112.65	110.59
1991-92	102.86	137.55	127.64
1992-93	123.89	145.65	140.75
1993-94	149.04	177.91	155.91
1994-95	158.25	162.50	136.20
1995-96	188.42	209.01	182.96
1996-97	205.62	324.40	186.94
1997-98	197.82	253.64	195.22
1998-99	280.34	299.95	235.15
1999-00	337.44	356.04	234.32
2000-01	435.00 (R.E.)	448.64 (R.E.)	309.22 (R.E.)
2001-02	510.48 (B.E.)	498.18 (B.E.)	346.17 (B.E.)

Source: Budget in Brief, Government of Meghalaya, 1978-79; *Budget at a Glance,* Government of Meghalaya:: 1984-85; 1986-87; 1989-90; 1994-95; 1998-99; 2000-01; 2001-02.

Table 4.2(b) Sector-wise Revenue Expenditure of Nagaland (in crores)

Years	*General Receip ts*	*Social Services*	*Economic Servi es*
1963-64	1.08 (44)	0.70 (29)	0.65 (28)
1964-65	4.97 (58)	2.05 (24)	1.47 (18)
1965-66	5.83 (61)	2.79 (28)	1.16 (11)
1966-67	6.54 (50)	3.43 (26)	3.08 (24)
1967-68	7.10 (48)	4.20 (26)	3.46 (24)
1968-69	7.80 (41)	5.23 (27)	5.92 (32)
1969-70	9.69 (46)	6.42 (30)	4.77 (24)
1970-71	10.56 (43	7.03 (29)	7.01 (28)
1971-72	10.98 (38)	8.70 (30)	8.72 (32)
1972-73	12.26 (41)	9.56 (31)	8.56 (28)
1973-74	13.19 (42)	10.86 (35)	7.00 (23)
1974-75	13.53 (38)	11.49 (32)	10.47 (20)
1975-76	16.49 (39)	13.39 (31)	12.72 (30)
1976-77	16.39 (35)	13.86 (30)	16.21 (35)
1977-78	19.44 (36)	15.59 (30)	18.25 (34)
1978-79	25.34 (36)	24.23 (32)	24.26 (32)
Annual Plan 1979-80	24.48 (35)	21.36 (31)	22.67 (34)
1980-81	32.87 (36)	29.53 (32)	28.97 (32)

(Contd...)

Years	*General Receip ts*	*Social Services*	*Economic Servi es*
1981-82	34.15 (34)	30.46 (30)	36.03 (36)
1982-83	48.24 (38)	39.66 (30)	42.95 (32)
1983-84	64.78 (40)	48.45 (29)	51.98 (31)
1985-86	88.83 (38)	75.95 (33)	63.28 (29)
1986-87	103.05 (38)	79.75 (30)	85.90 (32)
1987-88	124.99 (38)	94.30 (28)	109.73 (34)
1988-89	130.91 (36)	102.42 (28)	131.75 (36)
1989-90	144.58 (38)	123.84 (32)	112.09 (30)
1990-91	143.97 (34)	119.81 (28)	156.69 (38)
1991-92	174.62 (36)	127.95 (26)	179.31 (38)
1992-93	163.01 (40)	129.04 (32)	109.26 (28)
1993-94	214.10 (40)	158.94 (29)	175.70 (31)
1994-95	280.62 (49)	168.79 (28)	135.21 (23)
1995-96	336.58 (40)	248.44 (29)	249.46 (31)
1996-97	352.90 (42)	242.56 (28)	251.84 (30)
1997-98	419.40 (41)	250.10 (25)	334.30 (34)
1998-99	463.80 (44)	279.30 (26)	306.00 (30)
1999-2000	540.20 (45)	326.00 (27)	314.10 (28)
2000-01	576.60 (45)	348.60 (27)	331.70 (28)

Sources: Finance Accounts of Nagaland 1963-64 to 1997-98; Statistical Abstract of Nagaland; CMIE, March 2001.

Note; Figures as shown within brackets are the average plan percentage of each sectorto total revenue expenditure of the state.

Column 2 of above Table indicates the revenue expenditures on social services. The relative share of total revenue expenditure under this head suggests that the social welfare oriented activities has remained an important programmes and policies of the respective state governments throughout. If developmental expenditure on social services will presumably be taken to reflect public expenditure on human capital then, experiences of these two states negate the above functional relationship as economic backwardness coupled with a reasonable degree of poverty make its presence felt in these states of North-Eastern region.

Column 3 of the table brings out the data of revenue expenditure on Economic Services. A close look at the above tables indicates that although there has been an increase in revenue expenditure under this particular head over the years, spectacular development in agriculture and allied services, industry and minining still remains a day dream for these regions of the North-Eastern part of the economy. in the later two plan periods.

We have made an attempt to calculate the exponential growth rate of revenue expenditure sector wise by following the similar procedure ($Y= ae^{rt}$). The results of the estimated equations are presented below for the two states.

	Nagaland	Meghalaya
1.	$G_S = 281.755\, e^{.142517t}$ $R^2 = .97$	$Gs = 4.2354e^{0.1578t}$, $R^2 = .9939$
2.	$S_S = 193.281\, e^{.145200t}$ $R^2 = .97$	$Ss = 4.6786e^{0.1593t}$, $R^2 = .9922$
3.	$E_S = 158.353\, e^{.154161t}$ $R^2 = .96$	$Es = 7.0426e^{0.1341t}$, $R^2 = .9877$

where, G_S = General Services;

S_S = Social Services;

E_S = Economic Services.

These results suggest that comparatively, the growth rate of revenue expenditure on economic services in Nagaland is higher, i.e. 15 per cent, whereas in case of Meghalaya, it is the social sector which accorded the highest priority. The growth rates further indicates that that over the years, the economic policy of the government of Nagaland has tilted towards the development of the agriculture and allied services, community development, power development and transport and communication. In contrast to it, economic policy in the state of Meghalaya has tilted towards the development of the service sectors over the years.

No doubt, that the revenue budget so far we discussed gives a partial picture of the aggregate resource utilisation position of the state governments. In order to have an in-depth understanding of the intricacies of the state resource utilisation, an analysis of the capital budget becomes imperative. This is what has been spelt out in the following paragraphs.

Table 4.3(a) Sector-wise Capital Outlay of Meghalaya

(Rupees in Crores)

Year	General Services	Social Services	Economic Services	% of (1) to TCO	% of (2) to TCO	% of (3) to TCO
0	1	2	3	4	5	6
1972-73	0.35	....	2.75	2.32	....	18.25
1973-74	0.27	....	3.21	3.69	....	43.91
1974-75	0.93	1.44	3.72	12.14	18.80	48.56
1975-76	0.46	1.61	5.12	5.69	19.90	63.29
1976-77	0.30	1.49	4.46	2.56	12.72	38.09
1977-78	0.71	2.02	5.99	4.44	12.63	37.44
1978-79	0.70	3.28	8.20	4.70	22.03	55.07
1979-80	0.70	6.95	8.65	3.84	38.10	47.42
1980-81	0.74	10.08	10.28	1.76	23.96	24.41
1981-82	1.52	9.46	12.42	2.44	15.19	19.94

(Contd...)

0	1	2	3	4	5	6
1982-83	2.24	10.17	13.91	5.64	25.62	35.05
1983-84	3.35	15.72	14.54	7.00	32.85	30.39
1984-85	3.04	11.39	16.71	4.94	18.53	27.18
1985-86	2.92	17.80	17.44	5.13	31.26	30.62
1986-87	4.95	22.03	24.34	6.71	29.85	32.99
1987-88	3.72	22.05	27.78	4.98	29.50	37.16
1988-89	6.44	21.48	33.06	6.89	22.98	35.37
1989-90	4.66	23.40	39.49	5.07	25.46	42.96
1990-91	6.32	23.52	45.11	6.66	24.79	47.54
1991-92	6.17	26.80	50.44	4.97	21.57	40.60
1992-93	5.84	31.66	65.08	3.28	17.76	36.50
1993-94	8.72	29.63	66.91	2.05	6.95	15.70
1994-95	5.10	29.07	68.65	1.50	8.57	20.24
1995-96	8.06	35.48	90.61	3.73	16.43	41.95
1996-97	6.08	46.38	72.39	3.09	23.59	36.82
1997-98	4.77	42.49	78.62	2.88	25.66	47.47
1998-99	5.98	50.13	88.39	2.88	24.16	42.60
1999-00	9.46	53.76	101.95	3.54	20.09	38.10
2000-01	12.97*	120.45*	125.65*	3.17	29.45	30.72
2001-02	14.49**	118.14**	132.80**	3.37	27.45	30.86

Note: * = Revised Estimate; **=Budget Estimate; TCO = Total Capital Outlay

Source: Budget a Glance, Government of Meghalaya:: 1974-75; 1977-78; 1984-85; 1989-90; 1994-95;1998-99;2001-02.

$Gs = 1.0892^{e0.1061t}$, $R^2 = 0.7823$

$Ss = 4.6786e^{0.1593t}$, $R^2 = 0.9922$

$Es = 7.0426e^{0.1341t}$, $R^2 = 0.9877$

The sector wise capital outlay exhibits some interesting results.

Table 4.3(B) Sector-wise Capital Outlay of Nagaland (in crores)

Year	General Services	Social Services	Economic Services	% of (1) to TCO	% of (2) to TCO	% of (3) to TCO
0	1	2	3	4	5	6
1963-64	0.5	0.10	0.31	10.86	21.73	67.41
1964-65	0.10	0.16	1.18	4.84	7.76	87.4
1965-66	0.11	0.19	3.63	2.80	4.83	92.37
1966-67	0.02	0.16	2.88	0.66	5.22	94.12
1967-68	0.05	0.20	6.07	0.8	3.16	96.04
1968-69	0.21	0.21	4.05	4.70	4.70	90.6
1969-70	0.24	0.67	4.59	4.36	12.18	83.46
1970-71	0.24	0.98	5.66	3.48	14.24	82.28
1971-72	0.23	0.68	8.49	2.44	7.23	90.33
1972-73	0.18	0.74	7.78	2.06	8.50	89.44
1973-74	0.26	0.46	6.73	3.48	6.17	90.35
1974-75	0.42	2.84	7.89	3.76	25.47	70.77
1975-76	0.54	2.98	7.93	4.71	26.02	69.27
1976-77	0.68	3.24	7.06	6.19	29.50	64.31
1977-78	0.33	3.87	11.54	2.09	24.58	73.33
1978-79	0.55	5.62	13.41	2.80	28.70	68.5
Annual Plan 1979-80	0.79	6.52	14.95	3.54	30.00	66.46
1980-81	0.92	7.79	16.99	3.57	30.31	66.12

(Contd...)

0	1	2	3	4	5	6
1981-82	1.19	8.79	17.84	4.27	31.6	64.13
1982-83	1.88	10.37	22.19	5.45	30.11	64.44
1983-84	3.40	13.01	20.66	9.17	35.09	55.74
1984-85	2.45	21.28	8.41	7.62	66.21	26.17
1985-86	5.07	17.01	22.39	11.40	38.25	50.35
1986-87	7.50	17.97	34.10	12.60	30.16	57.24
1987-88	8.73	19.27	46.21	11.76	25.96	62.28
1988-89	10.34	25.62	38.25	13.93	34.52	51.55
1989-90	9.20	30.85	45.39	10.76	36.10	53.14
1990-91	8.83	26.54	51.58	10.15	30.52	59.33
1991-92	10.44	27.67	58.81	10.77	28.54	60.69
1992-93	15.19	17.67	46.42	19.05	22.23	58.64
1993-94	9.09	27.15	59.93	9.45	28.23	62.32
1994-95	3.17	6.48	34.41	7.19	14.70	78.11
1995-96	11.93	30.41	101.40	8.30	21.15	70.55
1996-97	13.14	57.09	134.61	6.41	27.87	65.72
1997-98	16.50	74.00	94.90	8.90	40.00	51.1
1998-99	14.90	89.10	113.50	6.85	40.93	52.22
1999-2000	12.90	82.00	110.80	6.28	39.84	53.88
2000-01	12.90	77.30	99.50	6.80	40.74	52.48

Source: Finance Accounts of Nagaland; Statistical abstract of Nagaland; CMIE, March 2001.

$G_s = 4.9981\, e^{.17025t}$ $R^2 = .91$

$S_s = 16.8886\, e^{.1759t}$ $R^2 = .90$

$E_s = 181.473\, e^{.11472t}$ $R^2 = .89$

Although the total capital outlays on general services, social services and economic services have increased over the years, the increase in capital outlay on economic services was accorded with the highest priority followed by the social services. Capital outlay on general services is presented in Column 1 of the table and that indicates that the general services received the least attention in the state of Meghalaya where it is the economic services which received least treatment in Nagaland over the years. Column 1 of the table further exhibits a fluctuating trend of capital outlay on general services over the years.

Column 3 of the table presents the capital outlay on economic services. The above tables clearly indicates the priorities of the government for the development of agriculture and allied services, community development, transport and communication, housing, rural and urban development, public health and power development, etc. over the years.

In order to substantiate the above findings, we have calculated the percentage share of the sector-wise capital outlay to the total capital outlays and have presented the same in column 5, 6 and 7 of the above Tables. The percentage share of capital outlay on general services remained more or less static during the period as evident from column 5 of the table.

Whereas, the percentage share of capital outlay on social services showed a decreasing trend right from 1964-65 till the year 1973-74. Then, the percentage shares picks up to an upward trend from the year 1974-75 and remained almost static till 1990-91. Thereafter, the percentage share showed a downward trend from 1991-92 to 1996-97. Nevertheless, the percentage share of capital outlay on social services reported a considerable increase from 1997-98 and remained static till 2000-01 for the state of Nagaland. On the other hand, the percentage share of capital outlay on social services increased from the third plan average till the sixth plan average. But beginning from the seventh plan average, its percentage share started declining up to the eight-plan average. And in the following plan i.e. ninth plan average, its percentage share picks up to 40 per cent.

On the other hand, the percentage share of capital outlay on economic services exhibited an upward trend beginning from 1963-64 to the year 1973-74. The percentage share however remained at a lower level and remained almost static for the rest of the years i.e. from 1974-75 till the year 2000-01, the last year of our study. The plan average percentage share which was 89.30 per cent in the third plan average increased to 93.90 per cent in the following three year annual plan average i.e.1966-67 to 1968-69. Thereafter, its percentage share started declining in the rest of the plan periods except a minor increase in the two-year annual plan average i.e.1990-91 to 1991-92 and eight plan average. And finally, the percentage share saddled at 52.41 per cent in the ninth plan average.

4.5 Concluding Remarks

The above study clearly indicates that the capital outlay on public works in the states has not been consistent over the years. The social welfare services continue to remain an important activity of the states over the years. Although the capital outlay on economic services shared the substantial capital expenditure of the states in its real terms, there has been a persistent fluctuation of capital investment on this sector. Rather, a decreasing trend of its percentage share to total capital outlays has been the feature of capital investment on economic services. The repercussion effect can be visualised in terms of the slowing down of economic development in both the states.

Thus, to sum up, it may be argued that both the states follow more or less a similar pattern of resource mobilization and also a similar pattern of resource utilization although they have opted for different budgetary controls. Based on the findings of the analysis of the two representative states, it can be generalised for all the North-Eastern States that the patterns of resource mobilisation and their utilisation have renamed region specific. In other words, it can be argued that the pattern of resource mobilisation has renamed a logical off shoot of the degree of horizontal and vertical integration that these economics have attained over a period of time.

Given the resource constraints imposed on these states by their failures to mobilise adequate internal resources, a reprisal of the tax responsiveness in terms of its productivity and inherent have much current significance. This, we intend to accomplish in the next Chapter.

SECTION -V

EMPIRICAL ANALYSIS

5.1 Introduction

An analysis of the compositional pattern of North-Eastern States' tax revenue in the preceding chapter shows that, on its own resource mobilization front, the region has failed to attain a desirable level of financial self-reliance in general and that with respect to its own taxing power in particular, its performance is not satisfactory. As a result of which, the financial dependence of the state on the Union government has been on the increase in recent years. Further, the analysis carried out so far suggests that the North-Eastern states have made half-hearted tax efforts during the period under study as a matter of which the observed anomalies in the states' tax system has been the resultant out come in recent years.

5.2 Thrust of the Problem

All these observed trends noted above provide a solid ground for the necessity and the desirability of undertaking an analysis of the efficiency of the state tax measures. Accordingly, an attempt is made in this section to review the responsiveness and productivity of North-eastern States' tax system in terms of Elasticity and Buoyancy to measure the relative degree of efficiency of the states' tax measures on the one hand and to indicate the extent of additional tax efforts needed to increase the revenue of the government on the other hand. This, besides being essential for arriving at a proper assessment of the overall success of the state government's measure to increase tax revenue would enable the state authority to ascertain how the revenue potential of a given tax system has been realized. So the related questions that are touched upon in this context are:

(i) Whether the state governments have succeeded in evolving a tax structure characterized by strong built-in flexibility of tax revenue with respect to state income growth? If it is so, to what extent? If it is not then to what extent, it has relied excessively on discretionary changes to improve tax yields and

(ii) Which of the individual tax items of the state are responsible for the in elasticity of the states' structure and to what extent , the inelasticity of states' tax structure is responsible for the excessive dependence on the Centre.

The suitable explanation to the question raised under(i) is sought interns of estimating the buoyancy of all the states taxes of north-eastern states takes together. Further, an analysis of elasticity of state's taxes is believed to take care of the second question(ii) raised above.

Regression equations (26) and (27) as spelt out in details in chapter two are used to measure the buoyancy and elasticity coefficients respectively, of the total tax revenues and of the tax revenues of major tax groups. The equations are estimated for each of the selected items, by the method of ordinary least squares.

5.3. Buoyancy and Elasticity of North-Eastern States Aggregate Taxes

In this section, an attempt is made to measure the elasticity and buoyancy of all state's taxes of North-Eastern states and then the same exercise was done for direct taxes, indirect taxes and shared taxes respectively.

Regression equations (6) and (7) are used to measure the

buoyancy and elasticity coefficients respectively of the total tax revenues of the revenues of major tax groups. The equations are estimated for each of the selected items by the method of the least squares.

5.4 Buoyancy Estimates

The income responses of the taxes are viewed in terms of their respective buoyancies which give an idea about the overall variation in tax revenue realizations comprising the effects of both automatic response and, of the discretionary response, i.e. the increase in tax yields attributable to additional taxation efforts.

Buoyancy estimates of the total tax revenue and of the selected tax groups covering the period 1963-64 to 2000-01 are presented in Table 5.1. The summary statistics R2, which measures the extent to which the total variations in tax revenues are systematically correlated with changes in State Income, is also presented.

Table 5.1 reveals that Tripura recorded the highest buoyancy coefficient (1.6374) in case of the states' total tax revenue. It is observed that buoyancy coefficients are greater than one in case of all the states for the states' total tax revenue. The buoyancy coefficient for the total own tax revenues works out as 1.2768 for the state of Tripura, which means over the period under review, every one percent increase in State Income on an average is associated with 1.437 percent increase in tax collections. A relatively lower buoyancy coefficient is observed for the states of Arunachal Pradesh, Nagaland and Manipur. This relatively lower response coefficient during the period under review suggests that the lower tax yields are on account of insignificant efforts made by the respective state governments to modify the tax structure during the periods towards additional resource mobilization.

Comparing States' own total tax revenue and shared

taxes, we found that the buoyancy coefficient is slightly more for shared tax revenue than that for States' own total tax revenue for the period 1963-64 to 2000-2001. This indicated that the changes in State's Net Domestic Product (NSDP) led to larger increase in State's share in Union taxes than in State's own tax revenue.

A perusal of Table 5.1 also indicates that the major reason for higher degree of buoyancy of shared taxes is the substantial efforts put in by the Union Government in particular. Further, Table 5.1 discloses that the direct taxes group in particular can mostly be held responsible for the poor aggregate tax yields to certain extent. Between the two aggregate yields - direct taxes and indirect taxes - the responses exhibited by the latter are observed to be higher. In a relative sense, the buoyancy coefficients of direct taxes in case of almost all the states are relatively less than the buoyancy coefficients of indirect taxes. Further, the buoyancy coefficient of the total taxes on property and capital transaction has recorded relatively lower growth in all the states.

The observed trends of buoyancy coefficients do provide further evidence to one of the earlier inferences, viz., that the coefficients obtained in case of supposedly more elastic taxes (direct) is less than that of the supposedly inelastic (indirect) taxes. The low buoyancy coefficients of the taxes on property and capital tax group raises doubt about the feasibility of these taxes in the overall tax system of the State from the point of view of its economy and efficiency.

Given the theoretical explanation that the buoyancy of taxes should be significantly higher than unity, the overall picture of the North-Eastern states' tax yields appears to be less satisfactory in the sense that, on the whole, the buoyancy coefficients of all the major tax groups have stayed slightly above one and all the states under study experience more or less the similar trends.

Since the buoyancy coefficient takes into account both the automatic response as well as discretionary response of a tax or tax system, a simple comparison of these coefficients in different time periods is not a very meaningful measure of the relative efforts made by the State Government in mobilizing resources for the public sector over any given period. This necessitates for carrying out an analysis of elasticity, which has been set out in the following paragraphs.

5.5 Tax Elasticity

Tax elasticity measures the degree of automatic response of the tax yields to changes in state/national income after subtracting the discretionary response of a tax from the total response of the tax. A high tax elasticity over a period of time indicates the probable tax revenue that the government can raise with an unchanged tax rate and base of the tax or of the tax system. Elasticity coefficients of the total tax revenues as well as of sectoral tax groups are computed and presented in Table 5.2.

The table indicates that with respect to State Income, the elasticity of the State's total own tax revenue works out as of the order of 1.3682 for the period 1963-64 to 2000-2001in case of the state of Tripura. Assam emerged the second state in terms of its elasticity coefficient as regards to its total own tax revenue (1.2456). The elasticity coefficients of total own tax revenue was worked out to be lowest in case of the state of Nagaland (0.744). The low elasticity coefficients in case of Arunachal Pradesh,Nagaland and Manipur suggests that these States did not resort to any stringent discretionary measures to improve the tax yields during this particular period under study. The elasticities of the selected tax groups are rather divergent. Following one classification, they are ranging from 0.8567 for taxes on property and capital transaction in case of Nagaland to 1.1876 for the state of Assam. According to another classification they are ranging from 3.2390 for taxes on income and expenditure in case of the state of Nagaland to 1.10376 in case of Arunachal Pradesh. In general, direct taxes when compared to indirect taxes are rather less elastic. These elasticities thus give rise to follow up question, i.e., which particular taxes could mostly be identified as responsible for the observed lacuna in the major tax groups. Needless to say, this demands a further decomposition of the elasticities of the specified groups to the elasticities of the individual items of each group, which we have carried out in the last section of this chapter.

The overall elasticity of the North-Eastern states' tax system thus reveals that with every one percent increase in the State Income, the State's own taxes brought about a slightly more than one percent increase in the tax yields during 1963-64 to 2000-2001 all the states except the states of Nagaland and Arunachal Pradesh. It means that the system as a whole can be classified as adequately responsive type in all the states except the state of Nagaland and Arunachal Pradesh. .Where as the tax system in the case of Nagaland and Arunachal Pradesh can be classified as non responsive types. An efficient tax system ought to give better results and if it is progressive it should possess elasticity greater than one. From this angle, Nagaland's tax structure does not fare badly.

The performance of state's tax collections can mainly be accounted for the substantial growth of revenue from indirect taxation. And, the low elasticity of total direct taxes' revenue can mostly be attributed to the land revenue. Even on the theoretical ground, land revenue, because of the involved administrative and assessment difficulties, can be hypothesized as inelastic revenues.

The other interesting result is that the elasticities of the taxes on property and capital transactions and those of taxes on commodities and services are not differing to a significant extent in statistical sense in almost all the states.

A perusal of Table 5.3 indicates that on the direct taxes front, the additional taxation effort put in, is of minimal order. The difference between this group's buoyancy and elasticity is of the order of 0.1562 in case of Arunachal Pradesh and 0.0639 in case of Mizoram. The results also indicate that additional effort of al most all the states is non existence even in the case of indirect taxes. This clearly exhibits the lack of tax effort measures on the part of the state governments which can be identified as one of the factors responsible for a smaller and negligible difference obtained for the buoyancy and elasticity estimates of income and expenditure taxes. Further, the table indicates that the major reason for higher degree of buoyancy of commodity taxes is the substantial efforts put in by the State Governments particularly by the states of Nagaland and Manipur. This is substantiated by the figures of the net due to discretionary changes, which is of the order of 1.1812 and 0.3838 for the states of Nagaland and Manipur respectively.

A comparison of the estimates given in Table 5.1 with those provided by 5.2 discloses that over the period, the pattern of changes in tax yields is not uniform for all tax groups, while some tax groups have shown an improvement, others disclosed an opposite pattern.

5.6 Elasticity and Buoyancy of Individual State Taxes

The results of the preceding section revealed that over the years, the state has put a marginal effort to modify its direct tax structure to realize additional resources. And incase of indirect taxes, the state has absolutely not gone for any major discretionary changes in terms of an upward revision in its tax rate structure or in terms of the expansion of the base of various taxes. As such, additional resource mobilization has remained sluggish. They also disclosed that State's shared taxes are mostly responsible for the better performance in the revenue mobilisation. On the other hand, further decomposition of direct and indirect taxes suggests that taxes on property and capital transaction and taxes on commodities are less elastic in comparison to taxes on income and expenditure. These elasticities and buoyancies, thus give rise to the question, i.e., which particular taxes could mostly be identified as responsible for the observed lacuna. Accordingly, an attempt is made in the subsequent paragraphs to give a suitable reply to the question raised above.

The buoyancy and elasticity of North-Eastern region's individual taxes are estimated by the same procedure as used earlier in case of all taxed combined. However, instead of using the State Domestic Product as the explanatory variable in all cases, the output of particular sectors of the economy is substituted where appropriate. For example, given that the base of Land tax, it is not the entire State Product, but that of the State Domestic Product originating in the farming segments of the economy. In estimating the buoyancy and elasticity of the agricultural income tax, the State Domestic Product originating in the agricultural sector was taken as the explanatory variable. Elasticity and Buoyancy coefficients of the State's individual taxes are presented in Table 5.4.

It is evident from Table 5.4 that, of all taxes collected by the various Governments, taxes on income and expenditure is most responsive to changes in the State Income in comparison to all other state taxes. Further, looking at the elasticity coefficient, it is evident that only two taxes, viz. taxes on income and expenditure and professional tax have got elasticity coefficient greater than one in almost all the states. Similar observations are made as regards to state excise duty and sales tax. Over the years, any additional resource mobilisation has been effected out of these taxes due to the increase in state Domestic Product. The performance of these taxes may be judged as satisfactory by elasticity criteria in the sense that the government has accorded a built-in-flexibility to these two taxes. On the other hand, the elasticities State entertainment tax and land revenue are found to be very small and insignificantThe buoyancy coefficient of these taxes is worked out to be 0.379, 0.819, 0.00913 and 0.115 respectively. The buoyancy coefficients of these taxes incidentally happen to be low. Thus it may be inferred from the above findings that entertainment tax and land revenue can mostly be held responsible for the sluggishness of the tax revenue yields to the state government.

5.7 Concluding Remarks

From the overall trends that emerge from our analysis of elasticity and buoyancy of the major tax groups, we may draw the following inferences.

(i) On the direct tax front, the States have not succeeded in evolving a tax structure characterized by a strong built-in responsiveness of tax revenues with respect to State Income. In fact, these conclusions also lend adequate support to the earlier inference: in North-Eastern States, the supposedly elastic taxes in effect are less elastic. In contrast to the elasticity coefficient, the buoyancy coefficient worked out to be relatively greater, thereby substantiating the fact that the Government put relatively a greater degree of tax efforts to mobilize adequate resources from this source.

(ii) Indirect tax groups have shown constantly higher elasticity coefficient for the period under study. In contrast to it, the buoyancy coefficient for the years 1983-84 to 2000-2001 exhibits a contrasting result. It is observed that during this particular phase, the buoyancy coefficient of this group taxes remained at a extreme lower rate. The elasticity coefficient for this group's taxes for the same period is much higher than the buoyancy coefficient. This provides a solid ground to argue that during this period, the government's effort to modify its tax structure towards additional (own) resource mobilization has been marginalized. These higher elasticity coefficients have come into vogue on account of the indirect taxes' better responsiveness to the changes in the economic development of the State. This is evident from the figures on Net Due to Discretionary changes. And lastly,

(iii) Further decomposition of direct and indirect tax groups into major three groups namely, taxes on property and capital transaction, taxes on income and expenditure, and taxes on commodities and services gives us some contrasting results. In case of taxes on property and capital and taxes on commodities, the elasticity coefficient worked out to be rather low in comparison to taxes on income and expenditure. On these accounts, we may conclude that the state has not succeeded in evolving a tax structure in case of these taxes (taxes on property and capital transaction, and taxes on commodities), which can be characterized by a strong built-in-flexibility of the tax revenue to changes in state income.

TABLE 5.1 BUOYANCY ESTIMATES OF SELECTED GROUPS OF TAXES FOR THE PERIOD 1972-73 TO 2000-2001.

Tax Groups	States													
	Assam		Arunachal Pradesh		Mizoram		Nagaland		Tripura		Meghalaya		Manipur	
	Buoyancy Coneffícient	R2	Buoyancy Coneffícient	R2	Buoyancy Coneffícient	R2	Buoyancy Coneffícient	R2	Buoyancy Coneffícient	R2	Buoyancy Coneffícient	R2	Buoyancy Coneffícient	R2
State's Total Taxes	1.4513 (14.682)	0.9562	1.1027 (17.6951)	0.9572	1.3459 (9.8360)	0.8973	1.437 (34.755)	0.971	1.6374 (16.4381)	0.9044	1.3091 (13.6854)	0.9038	1.1353 (8.9470)	0.9252
State's Own Taxes	1.2131 (54.7322)	0.9639	1.0146 (5.4267)	0. 9228	1. 2044 (20.4763)	0.8756	1.061 (27.416)	0.954	1.2768 (21.4372)	0.8432	1.1671 (16.3672)	0.8568	1.01127 (18.4572)	0.9154
Direct Taxes	1.1074 (28.0058)	0.9664	0.7210 (3.8983)	0.7548	1.0266 (6.7849)	0.8904	1.023 (34.183)	0.970	1.1105 (10.3970)	0.9247	1.1256 (24.2967)	0.9220	1.0048 (16.4228)	0.8460
Indirect Taxes	1.2147 (4.7682)	0.9606	0.9206 (54.2859)	0.8820	1.2157 (13.6277)	0.9520	1.141 (16.128)	0.878	1.3126 (6.8224)	0.8894	1.2475 (5.8428)	0.9426	1.1458 (12.7682)	0.9355
Shared Taxes	1.4042 (5.9166)	0.8664	1.2356 (7.3086)	0.9446	1.2430 (18.8492)	0.8905	1.683 (26.580)	0.952	1.8763 (13.2565)	0.9065	1.4256 (7.4486)	0.9663	1.7956 (10.6642)	0.8684
Taxes on Capital Transaction	1.3044 (24.7660)	0.9020	0.9845 (4.8226)	0.8440	1.0225 (16.3262)	0.9216	1.277 (14.651)	0.856	1.2055 (6.95770)	0.9462	1.2400 (11.2582)	0.8826	1.2257 (18.4275)	0.9066
Taxes on Income and Expenditure	1.3784 (34.4227)	0.7856	1.0205 (9.7052)	0.9147	1.2704 (46.1125)	0.9446	1.760 (17.161)	0.891	1.3743 (8.9062)	0.8655	1.3364 (7.8491)	0.9048	1.4274 (6.2251)	0.9378
Taxes on Commodities	1.2906 (16.6058)	0.9562	1.1245 (6.7488)	0.8479	1.3755 (22.8401)	0.9447	1.288 (15.058)	0.863	1.4408 (17.4856)	0.9461	1.3942 (8.9452)	0.9644	1.4782 (7.0275)	0.8942

Note : Figures in the parentheses represents 't' values of the regression coefficient.

TABLE 5.2 ELASTICITY ESTIMATES OF SELECTED GROUPS OF TAXES FOR THE PERIOD 1972-73 TO 2000-2001.

	States													
	Assam		Arunachal Pradesh		Mizoram		Nagaland		Tripura		Meghalaya		Manipur	
Tax Groups	Buoyancy Coneffictient	R2	Buoyancy Coneffictient	R2	Buoyancy Coneffictient	R2	Buoyancy Coneffictient	R2	Buoyancy Coneffictient	R2	Buoyancy Coneffictient	R2	Buoyancy Coneffictient	R2
State's Total Taxes	1.2456 (32.8340)	0.9227	0.8674 (8.2284)	0.9082	1.2178 (7.9250)	0.9273	0.744 (56.824)	0.989	1.3682 (8.6647)	0.9466	1.1174 (9.8266)	0.9450	1.0052 (12.7850)	0.9087
State's Own Taxes	1.1028 (11.4682)	0.9458	0.9124 (6.8840)	0. 9668	1. 0657 (9.6681)	0.8944	1.008 (12.836)	0.9836	1.0952 (11.3374)	0.9860	1.0389 (12.7289)	0.9162	0.8956 (18.4572)	0.9154
Direct Taxes	1.0045 (16.7740)	0.8948	0.5648 (9.7604)	0.8868	0.9627 (22.7357)	0.9468	0.913 (641.681)	0.9889	1.0176 (14.1104)	0.9447	1.0020 (28.2697)	0.9664	0.9273 (6.7443)	0.9740
Indirect Taxes	1.1042 (8.2488)	0.9040	0.8006 (44.8022)	0.8602	1.0682 (14.5542)	0.9660	1.1560 (281.797)	0.9720	1.0965 (16.4684)	0.9602	1.0477 (42.5747)	0.8957	1.0037 (9.0642)	0.9080
Shared Taxes	1.2062 (7.4611)	0.9406	1.0466 (12.0728)	0.9092	1.0228 (8.5667)	0.9782	0.5392 (26.580)	0.945 7	1.4023 (12.7730)	0.9226	1.1863 (8.3310)	0.9059	1.4260 (9.1066)	0.8982
Taxes on Capital Transaction	1.1876 (6.8477)	0.9660	0.9217 (9.8260)	0.8864	1.0001 (18.7264)	0.9506	0.8567 (23.723)	0.9408	1.1027 (11.6827)	0.9462	1.1084 (16.3602)	0.9628	1.0254 (13.5070)	0.9440
Taxes on and Income Expenditure	1.3672 (22.8043)	0.7856	1.0376 (10.6566)	0.9627	1.0968 (28.6468)	0.9068	3.2390 (126.717)	0.9980	1.1628 (9.4026)	0.9046	1.1488 (12.4228)	0.9265	1.1464 (8.3306)	0.9056
Taxes on Commodities	1.0296 (10.6332)	0.9462	1.0886 (16.2647)	0.9220	1.1084 (36.3956)	0.9620	0.1068 (2.166)	# #	1.2013 (7.5824)	0.9461	1.1672 (10.5866)	0.9010	1.0944 (18.5609)	0.9155

Note : Figures in the parentheses represents 't' values of the regression coefficient.

#We are not presenting these equations because they are not at all reliable due to small R2. Net due discretionary measures has been calculated by taking the difference of Buoyancy and elasticity Coefficient.

Table 5.3 Net Due to Discretionary Changes (Buoyancy Coefficientns Minus Elasticity Coefficients) 1972-73 to 2000-2001

	States						
Tax Groups	Assam	Arunachal Pradesh	Mizoram	Nagaland	Tripura	Meghalaya	Manipur
State's Total Taxes	0.2057	0.2353	0.1281	0.693	0.2692	0.1917	0.1301
State's Own Taxes	0.1104	0.1022	0.1387	0.053	0.1816	0.1281	0.11567
Direct Taxes	0.1029	0.1562	0.0639	0.110	0.0929	0.1236	0.0775
Indirect Taxes	0.1105	0.1200	0.1475	-0.015	0.217	0.1998	0.1421
Shared Taxes	0.1980	0.1890	0.2202	1.1438	0.474	0.2393	0.3696
Taxes on Capital Transaction	0.1168	0.0628	0.0224	0.4203	0.1028	0.1316	0.2003
Taxes on Income and Expenditure	0.0112	-0.171	0.1736	-1.479	0.2114	0.1876	0.2810
Taxes on Commodities	0.2610	0.0359	0.2671	1.1812	0.2395	0.227	0.3838

Table 5.4 Coefficient Buoyancy (B), Elasticity (E) and Related Statistics of States Taxes in North-East 1972-73 to 2000-2001

	Assam	Arunachal P.	Mizoram	Nagaland	Tripura	Meghalaya	Manipur
1. State Excise	B.1.530	B.1.012	B.1.277	B.0.379	B.1.422	B.1.330	B.1.410
	E.1.367	E.1.280	E.0.969	E.0.0665	E.1.207	E.1.050	E.1.117
2. Sales Tax	B.1.204	B.0.941	B.1.243	B.0.819	B.1.298	B.1.373	B.1.262
	E.1.103	E.0.496	E.1.286	E.0.251	E.1.237	E.1.156	E.1.116
3. Vehicle Tax	B.1.320	B.0.844	B.1.258	B.0.521	B.1.067	B.1.387	B.1.108
	E.1.236	E.0.948	E.1.006	E.0.592	E.1.306	E.1.205	E.1.006
4. Entertainment Tax	B.1.263	. .	B.0.0462	B.0.00913	B.1.049	B.1.220	B.1.362
	E.1.104	. .	E.0.247	E.0.0445	E.1.178	E.1.004	E.1.216
5. Taxes on Income and Expenditure	B.1.460	B.0.740	B.1.216	B.0.929	B.1.164	B.1.261	B.1.165
	E.1.107	E.0.979	E.1.030	E.1.158	E.1.003	E.1.352	E.0.967
6. Prfessional Tax	B.1.284	B.1.005	B.1.118	B.0.831	B.1.187	B.1.926	--
	E.1.004	E.0.8629	E.1.054	E.1.469	E.0.9652	E.1.378	—
7. Land Revenue				B.0.115			
				E.0.393			
8. Stamps and Registration	B.1.063	B.0.655	B.1.002	B.0.642	B.1.370	B.1.526	B.1.272
	E.0.728	E.0.852	E.0.985	E.0.522	E.1.008	E.1.227	E.1.324

CHAPTER-VI

SUMMARY AND CONCLUSIONS

The present chapter is an attempt to present a comprehensive account of the major findings of the study. The important findings of the study are as follows.

An analysis of the percentage share of state's total tax revenue and shared taxes in the net state domestic product exhibited some disturbing results. The percentage of State's own tax revenue to net state domestic product, increased slowly over the years in case of both the states. If, we judge the performances of the State's own tax revenue on the basis of its contribution to State income, then the performances of the State's own tax revenue presents a poor picture altogether. From this point of view, the State's own tax revenue has been increasing at a very slow rate during the period of our study. If we visualize tax-income ratio as the simplest measure of tax burden or sacrifice then the analysis revealed that the ratio has marginally increased in both the states of Nagaland and Meghalaya implying thereby the existence of a static tax structure over the years. This only proves that the States of North-Eastern region fare rather poorly on this count.

The analysis of the ratio of the State's own tax revenue to the total tax revenues accruing to the State was an attempt to ascertain the degree of tax efforts of the government during these years. It is quite disheartening to note that the ratio has nearly remained stagnant during the period of our study. In the light of the above finding, we may conclude that the States had neither put in extra efforts in raising its own tax revenue in a much more efficient way nor had it made any sincere effort to tap more resources during the period covered by our study. We believe, this might have been one of the factors responsible for the explosive cycles of public expenditure growth.

From the above findings, we may be tempted to draw two inferences. First, in the absence of any cohesive additional domestic resource mobilization programmes, financing of ever increasing public expenditure has led to the dependency syndrome of the State on the Centre for higher grants-in-aid. Secondly, the non-existence of a vibrant tax structure in order to finance the increased volume of public expenditure has placed the State at the mercy of market forces in terms of public borrowings. Judged from the angle of sound fiscal ethics, the performance of the State government to this effect seems to be unreasonable.

In order to find out the extent of dependency of the State on the contribution of Central taxes, an analysis of the shared taxes in the total tax revenue of the State revealed that the shared taxes have increased in both the states on an average from 30.02 per cent in the year 1972-73 to 71.85 per cent in the year 1998-1999. A striking feature of the State's taxation as revealed by our analysis was the phenomenal increase in contribution of the shared taxes to the total tax revenue of the State. It was observed that over the years, there has been a continual outpacing of the State's own tax revenue by the shared taxes. This indicated that the relative importance of the State's own taxes has been much less than it has been in the case of shared taxes as a component of total tax revenue of the State during the period of our study. As a result, the States have cut a poor figure with regard to the efforts put in by it during the last thirty years of our study to mop up additional resources from its own sources. The increasing dependence of the State on the share of Central taxes might partly be due to the ever-increasing pressure of the State on the Central Government to widen the pool of shareable taxes and partly due to the greater in-built flexibility and in-built responsiveness that have been brought into these taxes thereby making them more elastic and buoyant than the State's own taxes.

From the above analysis, one could see the dismal performance of the State governments in generating adequate resources from the sources at its disposal. Hence, an attempt was made to analyze the amount of funds transferred from the Centre to the States in order to find out the extent of dependency of the State on the Union Government. The ratio of Union resources transferred to aggregate State's expenditure was 62.29 per cent in the year 1972-73 which increased to 63.65 per cent in the year 2001-02 for the state of Meghalaya. Whereas, Nagaland's experience shows that this ratio is around 78 percent. The State's share of divisible taxes and duties has increased both in absolute and in relative terms. This trend has brought about a plausible deleterious effect on the growth and sustenance of the resource mobilisation efforts of the States in recent times. Given the level of resource mobilization effort of the States and given its degree of dependence on the Centre, we can hypothesize that the State will continue to depend heavily on the Central transfers, in the years to come unless it goes for an immediate rationalization of its tax structure. Therefore, in the absence of additional means to mop up adequate revenue, the States of North-East are far from the goal of financial self-reliance.

Based on the above exercises, we may be tempted to conclude that, the trend observed from the pattern of the composition of the State's taxes is not at all warranted from the point of view of a healthy fiscal economy. The reverse would have been commendable in the context of the State's efforts at achieving self-reliance with regard to resource mobilization of adequate resources for implementing several developmental programmes.

The analysis of the average annual growth rates of total public expenditure, net state domestic product showed that over the years, the average annual rate of increase of total public expenditure has surpassed the average annual rate of increase of net state domestic product and per capita expenditure. The extraordinary growth of public expenditure in relation to the net state domestic product may be attributed to the massive involvement of the governments in their over all developmental activities of the state in the presence of a highly expanded service sector and a non-existence industrial sector. In the states where the average annual rate of growth of public expenditure tends to be near about double than the average rate of growth of net state domestic product, raises serious doubt about the productivity and efficiency of the public expenditure programmes in the face of a subsistence agricultural sector and low per capita income.

Further, the analysis on the revenue expenditure exhibited an increasing trend during the entire period covered by our study. When revenue expenditure was taken as a percentage to total public expenditure, it was found that for most of the years, revenue expenditure constituted on an average more than 70 per cent of total public expenditure. This increase of revenue expenditure of the State governments clearly exhibited the pattern and direction of public expenditure whereby the States had failed miserably in building up its capital base for further development. This clearly shows that over the years, a large chunk of public investment has entered into the unproductive channels, as it is evident from its high percentage share in net state domestic product.

The analysis of capital outlay as a percentage of total

public expenditure enabled us to find the trend of public investment taking place in the States during the period of our study. It was observed that capital expenditure on an average constituted less than 30 per cent of total expenditure for most of the years covered by our study. A distressing feature that emerged from the analysis was the declining trend of capital expenditure over the years. This only proves that the State has not been able to pursue expenditure policies in consonance with the achievement of long term goals and objectives.

The analysis of the pattern of public expenditure in the State of Meghalaya, based on the sector-wise analysis of revenue expenditure indicated that the expenditures on social services accounted for the maximum annual compound rate of growth of 15.93 per cent while the general services recorded 15.78 per cent and the economic services showed 13.41 per cent. The above growth rates indicate that the revenue expenditures on social services account for the maximum rate of growth followed by the revenue expenditures on general services and economic services. This has resulted in a disproportionate growth of the service sector. The disproportionate growth of the social sector has not only absorbed most of the public investment funds over the years, but also has given rise to a weaker linkage between the different sectors of the economy. The weak linkage is not a healthy sign from the point of view of sustainable economic development and also from the point of view of domestic resource mobilization. Similarly, the exponential growth rates of the sector wise revenue expenditure in the context of Nagaland exhibits that the state does not markedly differ from the state of Meghalaya.

From the above findings, it is clear that, as an instrument of resource mobilization, fiscal policy in general and the taxation policy of the State Government in particular has not been a remarkable success. From the available evidence, it is seen that taxation policy of the State both through its direct and indirect tax front has not able to bring about any significant increase in the overall resource mobilization programme to meet its ever increasing public expenditure programmes. As a result of which the dependence of the state on the centre is on the increase in recent years.

In this Section, an attempt is made to suggest certain policy implications in the light of the foregoing findings. So far our analysis exhibited a poor elasticity and buoyancy coefficients for the entire tax system of the North-Eastern states. The results no doubt support the state's inability to mobilize adequate resources internally for its various developmental purposes. To overcome the existing deficiencies, we hope the following policy prescriptions may help the state government to certain extent.

It is always possible to devise a suitable system of taxation where the existing weakness can be removed.

Taking into account the above factors, it is possible to suggest the following considerations for evolving a suitable system of taxation.

Given the high proportion of consumption expenditure in total State Domestic Product, the relative share of Government revenues has to be increased mainly by impinging upon consumption activities. This can be brought about by rationalizing the estisting taxes in the indirect tax group. Here, the emphasis will have to be on the concerted efforts of the state governments in devising a tax rate regime, which will take away a reasonable proportion of the incremental consumption expenditure into the tax net. Clearly, therefore, what we argue is that the incidence of taxation should be more on those sectors which, in the development process, enjoy a faster growth of incomes; and the particular instruments of taxation have to be tailored on such a way that they operate in these sectors most effectively.

Policy Implications

Given the basic objectives, the following elements may be mentioned as desirable for being incorporated in a satisfactory policy of taxation:

- In order to make the agricultural sector to bear a certain burden of cost of development, we propose a cess on agricultural land and also a cess on irrigation and power supply.
- The standard settlements should be periodically revised every five to seven years so as to make the agricultural tax system elastic with respect to changing economic conditions, and
- Lastly, we recommend a productivity linked professional tax on the large agricultural land owners. That the tax may be related to the reported annual income minus the cost of production. This to certain extent will help in regulating inter-sectoral flow of resources. As non existence of any tax in this sector facilitates the natural flow of resources between sectors.

On the indirect taxation front, we may stress on the Rationalization of simplification of the tax structure in order to compel it to be more buoyant and elastic than its original level. In this regards, certain measures which needs immediate attention are:

- The tax base of states' excise duty may be expanded by bringing more commodities under its fold. To achieve that, it is required that the state will have to reconsider its policy of prohibition.
- Further to make this tax more responsive and buoyant; we suggest a lower tax rate. Rationalization of tax rate structure may be carried out by substituting two or three tax rates for a number of tax rates.
- Ways have to be found to reduce the number of sales tax rate and levy uniform tax rates in respect of some

important commodities. The number of tax rates should be brought down to at least two or three in the course of next two years and this will no doubt reduce both administrative and compliance costs significantly.

- Measures should be taken to relieve the burden of the tax on inputs through a system of tax credits. And, with better information system, perhaps attempt could be made to extend the tax base to the stages beyond manufacturing on the principle of "value added".
- The sales tax incentives given for industrializations in the state need to be rationalized
- The other two taxes which need to be rationalized are the entertainment tax and stamps and Registration Duty. The levy of the stamp duties at very high rates of 15 to 20 percent has resulted in substantial under valuation of immovable property. This has led to investments in real estates an important source of underground economy. The same amount of tax could perhaps be collected by reducing the tax rate.
- The entertainment tax should be brought under stricter tax compliance in order to make it more buoyant and elastic. Further, we strongly recommend that a relatively greater progressive tax rate may be imposed on all sorts of entertainments and the tax rate may be considered as a percentage of the value of tickets .
- In case of the vehicle tax, we are tempted to make a suggestion that registration fee may be charged as a percentage of the value of the vehicle which should be made progressive. We think that this would bring a greater degree of built-in-flexibility and buoyancy not only to this particular tax but also to the indirect tax structure. The life time registration fee may be scrapped all together and in its place annual registration fee may be introduced.

- Every effort may be made to revise the tax rates of vehicle tax every five years by taking in to account the rate of inflation, the rate of increase in income.
- To make the professional tax as most viable direct tax, efforts should be made to expand the base and to bring more progression to the existing tax rate.
- lastly, we may propose the imposition of a poll tax if it is feasible as a alternative source to mobilize adequate resources for the state. The proposed tax will be a direct tax which will be levied on all the individuals at a flat rate. Since, it will be a tax on the mere existence of individuals and not on any economic base, the market distortion and the tax avoidance will be considered to be nil.

In addition to the above general recommendations to re-structure the North-Eastern region's tax structure, the following specific suggestions are considered to be tax responsive and tax buoyant.

Given the fact that in recent years, North-East economy is flooded with imported goods of all sorts from the neighboring countries, we strongly recommend:

- Import duty may be levied on all types of imported electronic goods, woolen blankets and materials, garments, dry fish, melamine products, footwear, imported soft drinks and cosmetics. This not only checks the flourishing parallel economy but also help in additional mobilization of resources to the state's exchequer.
- A levy in the form of additional user charges may be levied on two wheeler, four wheelers, tires and tubes, lubricants and other automobile spare parts.
- Toll gates may be made more vigilant to make the toll tax more tax yielding. Further, toll tax may be revised and progressivity should be brought in to it.
- An export duty may be imposed on the forest produce such as bamboo and timber.

- A high luxury tax may be imposed on the hotels and on long distance buses and Taxis.

We hope that if the above stringent taxation measure will be carried out, the government will be in a position to mobilize adequate revenue so as to bridge the gap in its budget deficits and to reduce its dependence on the centre.

If one were to attempt to compress our arguments in this work into one single argument, then, the problem of state finance has to be treated alongside the problems of societal needs and aspirations, societal attitude, cultural values, institutional value judgment, politics and public administration with a general sense of proportion. It is such an outlook on the part of the political and policy makers that can make it possible for them to come to grips with the problem which demands and will continue to demand attention in the state scene at all times to come. Formulation of fiscal policies should not be left to the political gimmick of the political parties that stay in power, but it should be left to the grounded realities of social and economic aspirations and concerns of the masses.

BIBLIOGRAPHY

Auld, D.A.L. (1971), "Automatic Fiscal Stabilizers: Problems of Identification and Measurement", *Journal of Public Finance*, Vol. 26, No. 4, pp.513-31.

Bagchi, A. and Sen, T. (1989), *Kerala's Revenue Potential : Projections for 1990-95*, National Institute of Public Finance and Policy, New Delhi.

Bagchi, Amaresh and Rao, M. Govnda. (1982), "Elasticity of Non-Corporate Income Tax in India", *Economic and Political Weekly*, Vol. 17 , pp. 1452-58.

Bahl, Roy W. (1971), "A Regression Approach to Tax Effort and Tax Ratio Analysis", *I.M.F. Staff Papers*, Vol.18.

Bansal, R.K. (1988), *Raising Additional Resources in the States*, Atlantic Publishers and Distributors, New Delhi.

Bretherton, R.F. (1937), "The Sensitivity of Taxes to Fluctuations of Trade", *Econometrica*, Vol. V, pp. 171-83.

Byrne, William J. (1983), "The Elasticity of the Tax System of Zambia 1966-1977" *World Development*, Vol. II, No. 2, pp. 153-62.

Chelliah, R.J. (1967), "Elasticity and Rate of Growth of State Taxes" in Joshi, M.D., (Ed).; *Mobilisation of State Revenues*, Impex India, New Delhi, pp. 49-53.

Chelliah, Raja J. and Sinha, Narian. (1983), *Measurement of Tax Effort of State Government 1973-1976*, National Institute of Public Finance and Policy, New Delhi.

Chelliah, R.J. (1969), *Fiscal Policy in Underdeveloped Countries*, George Allen and Unwin (Inida) Private Limited, Bombay.

Das, S.K. (1987), *Dynamics of Taxation in A Developing Economy (with special reference to Assam) : 1964-65 to 1978-79*, Omson Publication, Guwahati.

Easterly,W. and Rebelo, S. (1993) , "Fiscal policy and Economic growth:An Emperical Investigation, *Journal of Monetary Economics*,Vol.32.

Edelberg, V. (1940), "Flexibility of the Yield of Taxation : Some Econometric Investigation", *Journal of the Royal Statistical Society*, Part-II, pp.153-90.

Gandhi, Ved. P. (1970), *Some Aspects of India's Tax Structure*, Vora and Co. Publishers Pvt. Ltd., Bombay.

Groves, H.M. and Khan, C.H. (1952), "The stability of state and Local Tax Yields", *American Economic Review*, Vol. 41, pp.87-102

Hariss, R. (1968), *Income and Sales Taxes : The 1970 Outlook for States and Localities*, The Council of State Government, Chicago, pp.48-110.

Hicks, U.K. (1938), *Finances of British Government : 1920-36*, Oxford University Press, London.

Jain, M.M. (1969), "Income Elasticity of Indian Tax Structure 1955-56 to 1965-66", *Economic and Political Weekly*, Vol. IV, No. 18, pp.769-71.

Joseph, A. Pechman. (1953) *Yield of Individual Income Tax During a Recersion : Policy to Combet Depression*, Princeton University Press, Princeton.

Lakdawala, D.T. and Khambadkune, (1959), "The Sensitivity of Central Taxes : 1948-49 to 1954-55", *The Economic Weekly*, December 5th, pp. 1933-1940.

Legler, J.B., and Shapiro, P. (1968), "The Responsive of State Tax Revenue to Economic Growth", *National Tax Journal*, Vol. 21, No. 1, p. 47.

Lewis, W. Jr. ((1962), *Federal Fiscal Policy in The Post War Recersions*, D.C. Bar. Brookings Institution, Washigton.

Maxwell, J.A. (1955), *Fiscal Policy*, Henry Holt and Co., New York.

Musgrave Richard A. (1959), *The Theory of Public Finance*, Mc-Graw-Hill Book Co., New York.

Musgrave ,Richard A. and Miller, (1948), "Built in Flexibility",

American Economic Review, Reprint in *Readings in Fiscal Policy*, American Economic Association, pp.379-386.

Prest, A.R. (1969), "The Sensitivity of the Yield of the Personal Income Tax in the United Kingdom", *Economic Journal*, Vol. 72, pp. 576-596.

Purohit, M.C. (1995),"Reform of Union Excise Duties", *Economic and political Weekly*, Vol.XXX, No.21, pp.1255-59

Rao, K.B.K. (1969), "Income Elasticity of Central and State Taxes", *Margin*, Vol. 1, No. 3, pp.11-21.

Rao, M. Govinda. (1979), "Economic and Political Determinants of Sales Tax Revenue : A Case Study of Four State"', *Economic and Political Weekly*, Vol. XIV, No. 47, p.1925.

Rao, V.G. (1970), *The Responsiveness of the Indian Tax System 1960-61 to 1973-74*, Allied Publishers Pvt. Ltd., Banglore.

Reddy, K.N. (1975), "Inter-State Tax Effort", *Economic and Political Weekly*, Vol. X, No. 50, pp.1961-67.

Sahota, G.S. (1961), *Indian Tax Structure and Economic Development*, Asia Publishing House, Bombay.

Singer, N.M. (1968), "The use of dummy Variables in Estimating the Income Elasticity of State Income Tax Revenues", *National Tax Journal*, Vol. 21, No. 2, pp.200-04.

Singer, N.M. (1970), "Estimating State Income Tax Revenues : A New Approach", *Review of Economic and Statistics*, Vol. 52, pp.427-33.

Suresh, P.S. and Mishra, B. (2005),"Elasticity and Buoyancy: An Econometric Analysis

of Orissa's Tax System" *Journal of Social and Economic Policy*, Vo. 2, No. 2, pp. 131-147.

Thimmaaiah, G. (1984), *Perspectives on Tax Design and Tax Reforms*, Asia Publishing House, Dew Delhi.

Wasylenko, M. (March, 1975), "Estimating the Elasticity of State Personal Income Taxes", *National Tax Journal*, Vol. 28, No. 1, p.140.

Wilford, W.T. (1965), "State Tax Stability Criteria and the Revenue Income Elasticity Coefficient Reconsidered", *National Tax Journal*, Vol. 18, No. 3, pp.304-12.

INDEX

□□□